Contents

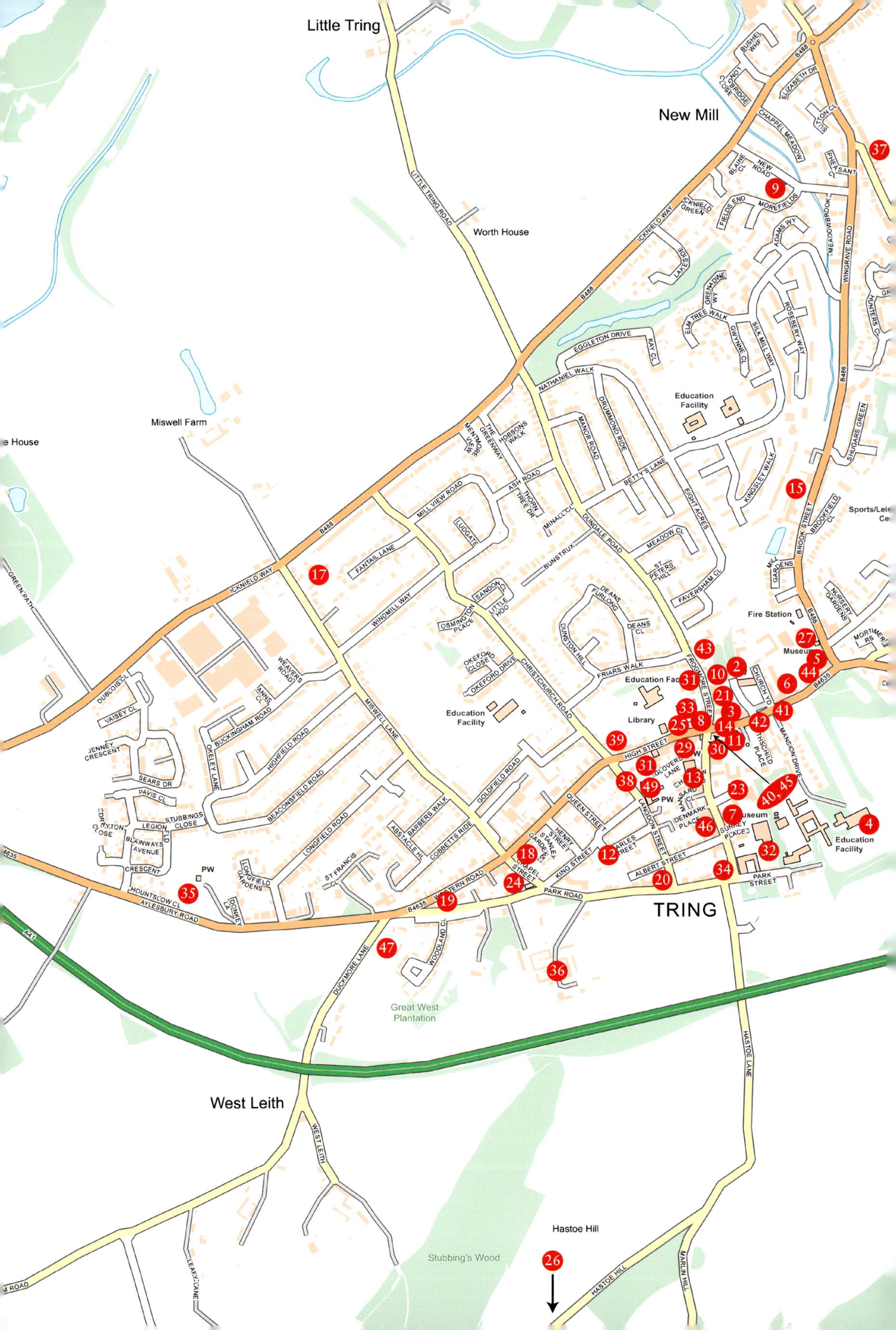

Little Tring
New Mill
Worth House
Miswell Farm
Education Facility
Library
Fire Station
Museum
Sports/Leisure Centre
TRING
Great West Plantation
West Leith
Hastoe Hill
Stubbing's Wood

TRING IN 50 BUILDINGS

PAUL RABBITTS

AMBERLEY

To the memory of William Huckvale, architect to the Rothschilds and who has left an incredible legacy of buildings in the town of Tring, in the county of Hertfordshire

First published 2024

Amberley Publishing, The Hill, Stroud
Gloucestershire GL5 4EP

www.amberley-books.com

British Library Cataloguing in Publication Data.
A catalogue record for this book is available from the British Library.

ISBN 978 1 3981 0490 7 (print)
ISBN 978 1 3981 0491 4 (ebook)

Typesetting by SJmagic DESIGN SERVICES, India.
Printed in Great Britain.

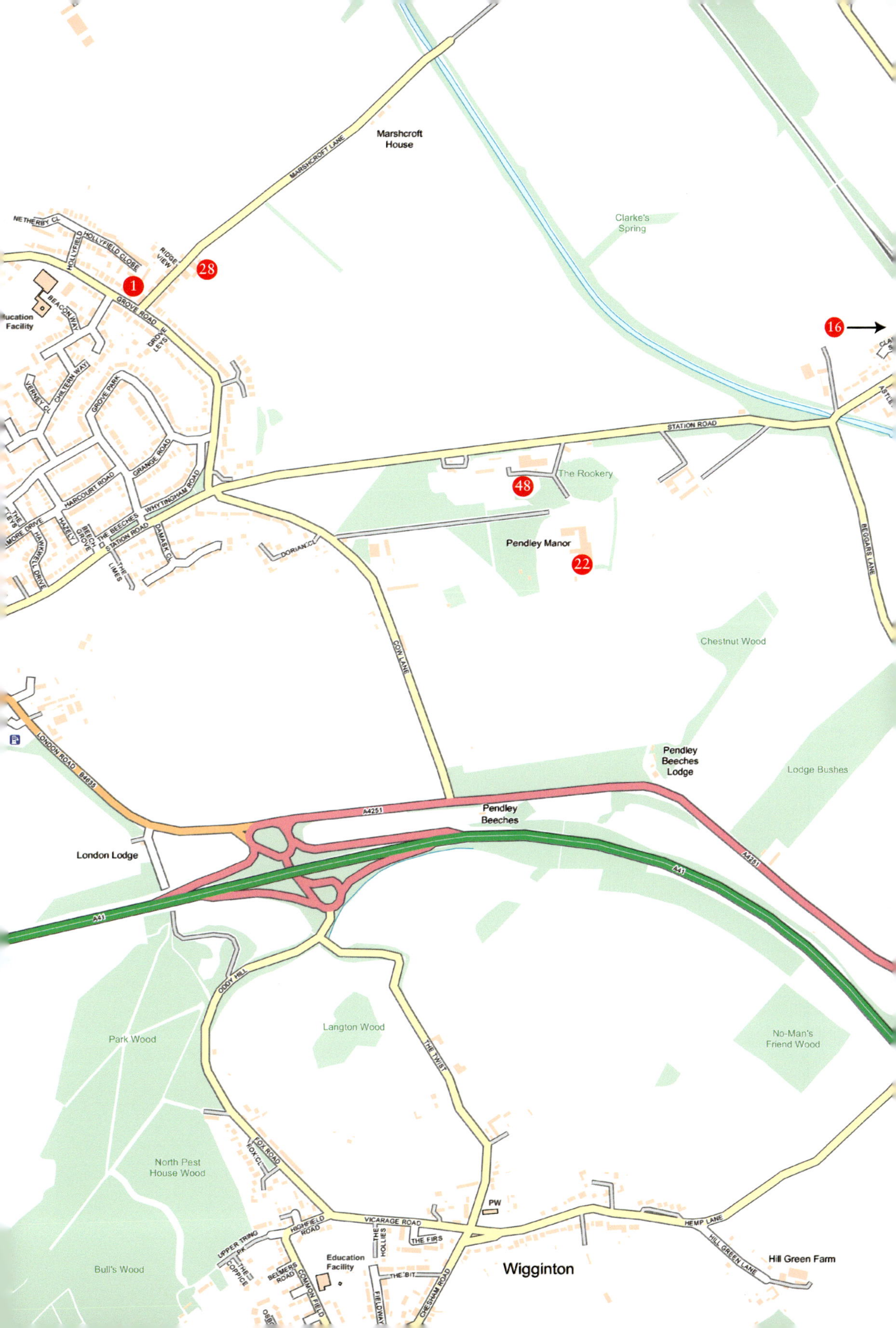

Marshcroft House
MARSHCROFT LANE
Clarke's Spring
NETHERBY CL
HOLLYFIELD CLOSE
HOLLYFIELD
RIDGE VIEW
28
1
GROVE ROAD
BEACON WAY
Education Facility
GROVE LEYS
16
CHILTERN WAY
VERNEY CL
GROVE PARK
GRANGE ROAD
HARCOURT ROAD
WHYTINGHAM ROAD
STATION ROAD
The Rookery
48
HAZELY
BEECH GROVE
THE BEECHES
STATION ROAD
DAMASK CL
THE LIMES
HAWKWELL DRIVE
DORIAN CL
Pendley Manor
22
BEGGARS LANE
COW LANE
Chestnut Wood
LONDON ROAD B4635
Pendley Beeches Lodge
Lodge Bushes
A4251
Pendley Beeches
London Lodge
A4251
A41
A41
ODDY HILL
Langton Wood
Park Wood
THE TWIST
No-Man's Friend Wood
North Pest House Wood
FOX ROAD
FOX CL
PW
HIGHFIELD ROAD
VICARAGE ROAD
HEMP LANE
UPPER TRING PK
THE HOLLIES
THE FIRS
HILL GREEN LANE
Hill Green Farm
Education Facility
Bull's Wood
THE COPPICE
BELMERS ROAD
COMMON FIELD
THE BIT
CHESHAM ROAD
FIELDWAY
Wigginton

Key

1. Old Grove Farm
2. Parish Church of St Peter and St Paul
3. The Bell Public House, High Street
4. Tring Park and Mansion
5. The Robin Hood, Brook Street
6. The Former Plough Inn, No. 50 High Street
7. Grace's Maltings, Akeman Street
8. The Former George Public House, Frogmore Street
9. New Mill Baptist Church
10. The Old Vicarage and Gatehouse
11. Former Brown's Brewery
12. King's Arms Public House
13. Baptist Chapel, Akeman Street
14. High Street Banks
15. The Silk Mill, Brook Street
16. Former Royal Hotel
17. Goldfield Mill
18. The Anchor Public House, Western Road
19. The Former Britannia Public House, Now Norfolk House, Western Road
20. The Castle, Park Road
21. Vestry Hall, Church Yard
22. Pendley Manor
23. Brown's Maltings
24. Church of St Martha
25. Grace Ironmongers, No. 68 High Street
26. Hastoe Village Hall
27. Former Cattle Market Buildings, Brook Street
28. Marshcroft Lane
29. Former Post Office, High Street
30. Victoria Hall, Akeman Street
31. Former Baptist Chapel, Frogmore Street, and New Baptist Church, High Street
32. Tring Zoological Museum
33. Constitutional Club/Conservative Club
34. Louisa Cottages
35. Tring Cemetery
36. Home Farm
37. The Manse, Grove Road
38. Ardenoak House
39. The Old Church House
40. The Market House, High Street
41. The Counting House
42. The Former Rose and Crown Hotel
43. The Black Horse, Frogmore Street
44. Former Unity Hall, Lower High Street
45. Tring Police Station
46. The Former Empire Picture Theatre, Akeman Street
47. Great West Plantation, Duckmore Lane
48. The David Evans Court Theatre
49. Corpus Christi Catholic Church
50. Tring School

Introduction

Bettley, Pevsner and Cherry, in the latest edition of *The Buildings of England: Hertfordshire*, describe Tring as follows: 'Although Tring has a long history, as the church demonstrates, its present character owes much to the Rothschild family and the local architect whom they favoured, William Huckvale (1848–1936).' The Rothschilds had bought land at Mentmore, across the border in Buckinghamshire, building Mentmore Towers to the design of Sir Joseph Paxton in 1836, followed by property in Aston Clinton and Halton; then in 1872 Lionel Rothschild bought Tring Park, intended for his eldest son Nathaniel, created 1st Baron Rothschild in 1885. Champneys was purchased in 1899 as a dower house, although it was never used as such. The association with the town continues; Jacob, the 4th Baron, is still lord of the manor. Rothschild buildings by Huckvale dominate the High Street, and remind residents and visitors of the important Rothschild connection.

Tim Amsden, from the Tring and District Local History and Museum Society, has studied architect William Huckvale for an intended biography. Huckvale was born in Camberwell, Surrey, in 1848 and was articled to a London firm of architects. In his early twenties he moved to Tring, and came to the attention of Alexander Parkes, agent to Tring Park Estate, and was commissioned to design some cottages. The volume of work greatly increased when Richardson Carr succeeded Parkes as agent and over forty years the majority of farms on the estate were rebuilt and many new cottages built throughout the area, including fifty which were presented to Tring Urban District Council.

Nathaniel, 1st Lord Rothschild, had very advanced ideas for his time and the farms and cottages were built to very high standards with piped water and proper sanitation. A few even had electricity supplied from a power station in the Silk Mill. Huckvale worked in the 'Old English', or Domestic Revival, style, which had been popularised by architects such as Richard Norman Shaw; this was a forerunner of the better-known Arts and Crafts school. With much use of timber-framing, tall chimneys and sweeping tiled roofs, Huckvale combined traditional vernacular features with modern planning to ensure health and hygiene.

As well as estate work in Tring, including the zoological museum, the cattle market and the Rose and Crown Hotel, he designed civic buildings like the Market House and the Victoria Hall, as well as many shops and private houses. His crowning achievement was the large house and estate village of Ashton in Northamptonshire, built for Lord Rothschild's younger son, Charles. With the

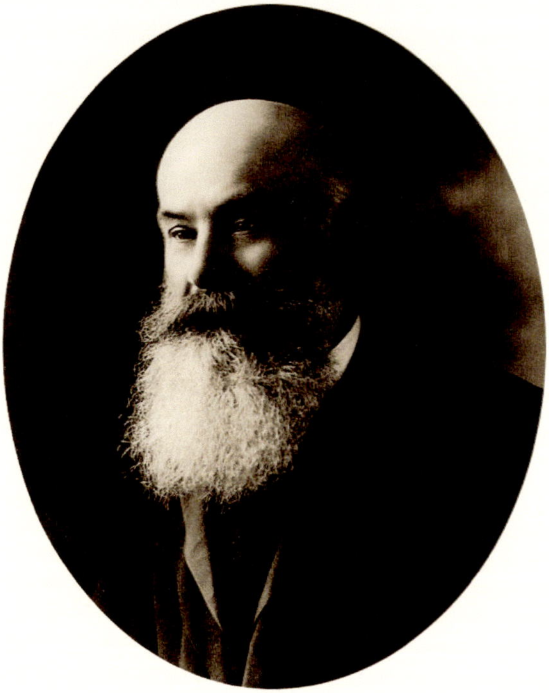

William Huckvale (1848–1936), architect to the Rothschilds. (© Tim Amsden)

outbreak of the First World War, closely followed by the death of Lord Rothschild in 1915, his career came to an end. William Huckvale died in Tring in 1936, aged eighty-eight, and is buried at Tring Cemetery, which he had himself designed. His son Will (1884–1965) was also an architect and designed several houses in Tring, notably in Station Road.

The 50 Buildings

1. Old Grove Farm

One of the oldest buildings in Tring is the original Tring Grove farmhouse on the corner of Marshcroft Lane, now named Old Grove Farm, which is one of the best examples in north-west Hertfordshire of a crown-post house used as a domestic dwelling. It is reputed to have been built between 1380 and 1480 with a late seventeenth-century rear wing. Many alterations have been made over the years, including the dividing of the building into three cottages for farm labourers. It is now a single dwelling.

This building served as the farmhouse for Tring Grove Farm up to about the end of the nineteenth century when a new and larger farmhouse was erected on the north side of Marshcroft Lane. In the 1920s it was occupied by the Halstead family until they emigrated to Canada in 1931. During the following years, this property was modernised and tenanted by farm workers, and was later sold as a private house to a Mr Rutland, followed by a Mr Figg when further alterations were made.

Converted into a single dwelling but maintaining its rustic charm.

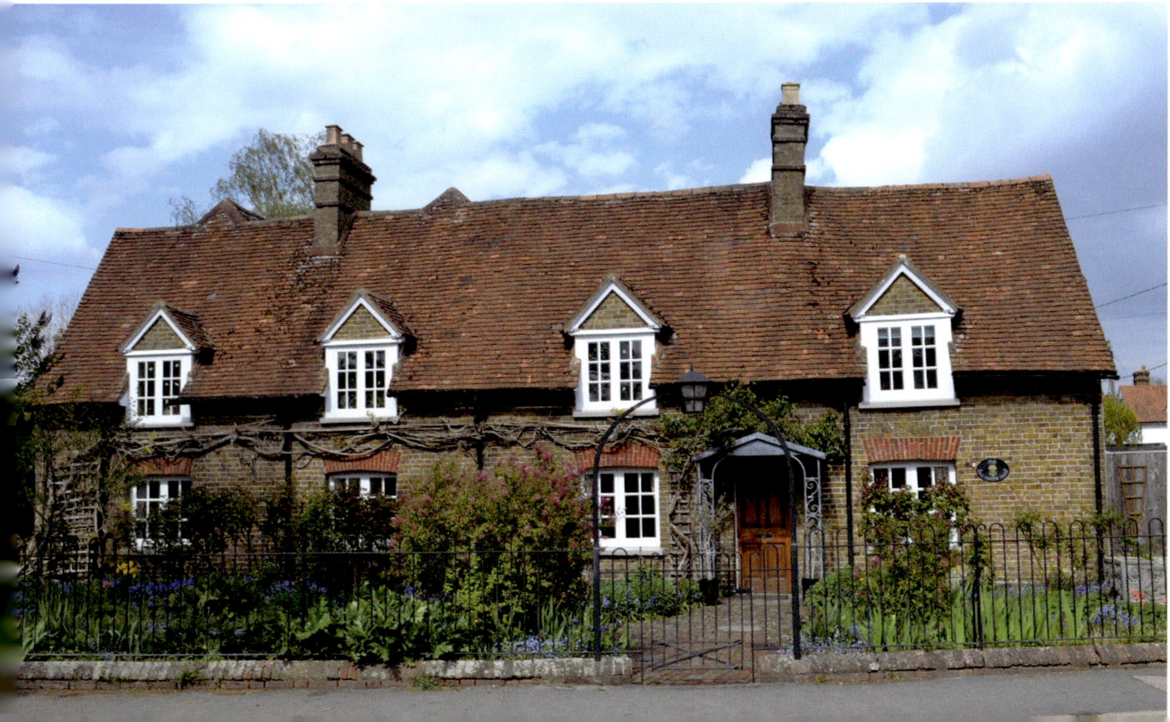

2. Parish Church of St Peter and St Paul

The church of St Peter and St Paul in the heart of Tring is over 700 years old, with its register dating from 1566. It is built of knapped local flint, and stone from the nearby village of Totternhoe. Its rather quaint spire at the centre of the tower is known as a Hertfordshire spike. Like many churches of today, little remains of what was the original building on the site, if anything at all. The original church here almost certainly predated the Norman Conquest. The church we see today though retains the shape and a number of interesting features from the fifteenth-century building. The pillars that form the arcades are copies of the originals which unfortunately had started to decay. The arches are original though, as are the wonderful stone corbels of fantastic creatures which separate them.

The church contains many interesting monuments throughout the building. This includes that of Sir William and Lady Gore of Tring Park. Sir William is shown wearing the robes of the Lord Mayor of London. Less obvious is one to Mary Anderson of Pendley Manor, with the coffin lid on the floor of the north aisle, which dates from 1200. The churchwarden pews are unusual as they have been raised to improve the view from them and above them are two painted panels depicting Moses and Aaron. These were donated to the church by William Gore in around 1715.

The parish church of St Peter and St Paul.

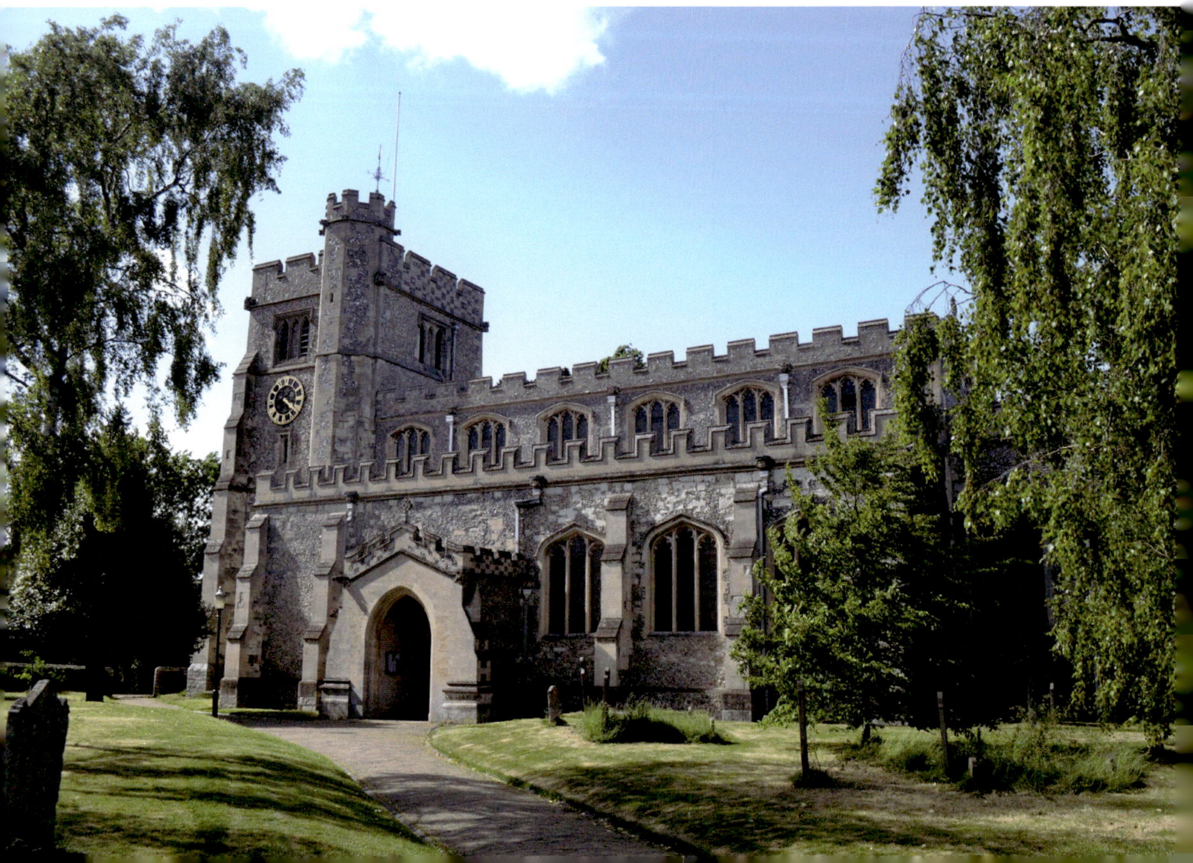

The uppermost part of the church is the belfry, which houses eight bells. Kelly's Directory of 1882 describes them: 'The church contains six bells dating from 1624–1882, the interior thoroughly restored in 1862 and partially rebuilt in 1880 and 1881. A new clock, chiming the quarters was placed in the tower at the same time. The restoration including two new bells, was finished in March 1882, at a cost of about £3,500, furnished by voluntary contributions. The pews in the nave were made in the 1860s by James Forsyth of London, as was the pulpit given by former patrons, the students of Christ Church College, Oxford.'

The choir stalls, screen and painting on the chancel roof were designed by well-known architect George Frederick Bodley (1827–1907). Bodley was an English Gothic Revival architect and was a pupil of Sir George Gilbert Scott, a relative by marriage, under whose influence he became imbued with the spirit of the Gothic Revival. Bodley became known as the chief exponent of fourteenth-century

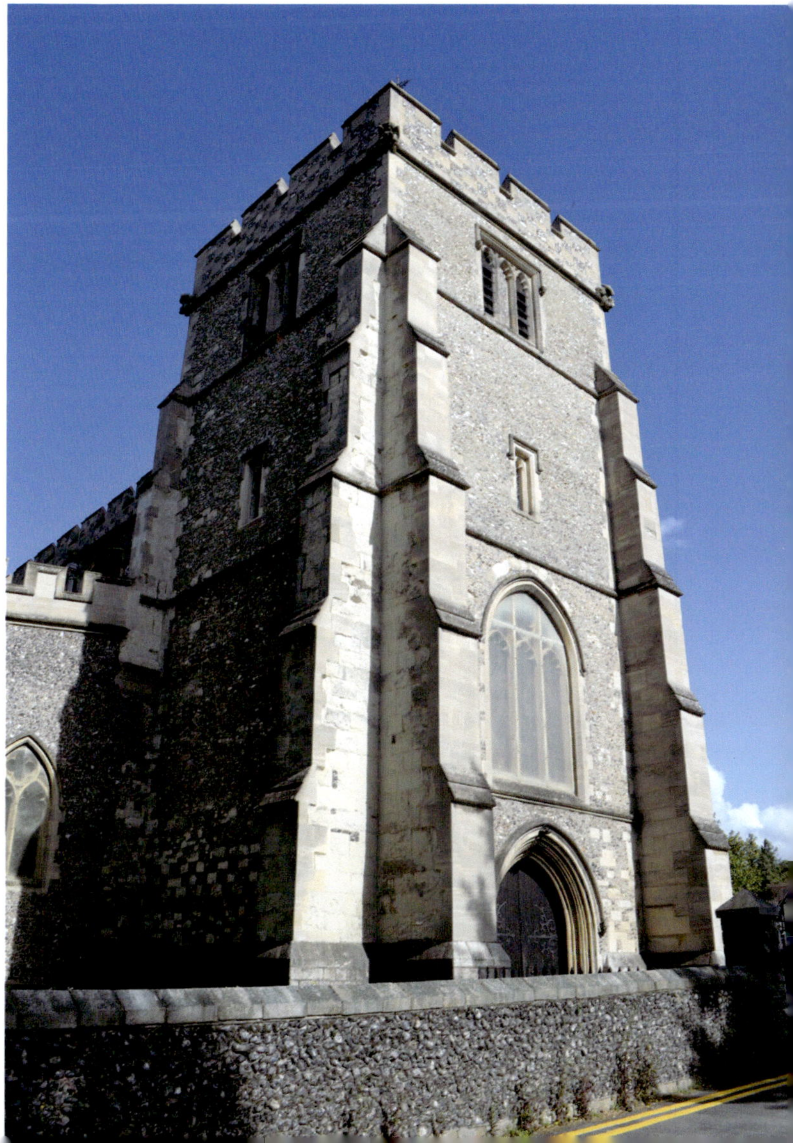

The tower contains six bells dating from 1624 to 1882 and two later additions in 1882.

English Gothic, and the leading ecclesiastical architect in England. Many of the stained-glass windows in the church are by the Victorian firm C. E. Kempe.

Charles Eamer Kempe (1837–1907) was a British Victorian-era designer and manufacturer of stained glass. His studios produced over 4,000 windows and also designs for altars and altar frontals, furniture and furnishings, lychgates and memorials that helped to define a later nineteenth-century Anglican style. The list of English cathedrals containing examples of his work includes Chester, Gloucester, Hereford, Lichfield, Wells, Winchester and York. Kempe's networks of patrons and influence stretched from the royal family and the Church of England hierarchy to the literary and artistic beau monde.

Other stained glass within the east window and the south-east one are by the well-known firm Clayton and Bell. They were one of the most prolific and proficient British workshops of stained-glass windows during the latter half of the nineteenth century and early twentieth century. The partners were John Richard Clayton (1827–1913) and Alfred Bell (1832–1895). The company was founded in 1855 and continued until 1993. Their windows are found throughout the United Kingdom, in the United States, Canada, Australia and New Zealand.

Clayton and Bell's commercial success was due to the high demand for stained-glass windows at the time, their use of the best-quality glass available, the excellence of their designs and their employment of efficient factory methods of production. They collaborated with many of the most prominent Gothic Revival architects and were commissioned, for example, by John Loughborough Pearson to provide the windows for the newly constructed Truro Cathedral.

3. The Bell Public House, High Street

Probably the oldest public house in Tring is The Bell, which remains on the High Street. It was certainly in existence in the early part of the seventeenth century as it was reported in 1611 that 'Henry Geary was before the Justices for keeping The Bell without a licence and a few years later for drunkenness.' In the 1660s tokens were issued by Mr Hastings Parrot of the Bell, as small change was in short supply. A Trade Directory, well before the first census return of 1801, lists Edward Jackson as the landlord, but by 1841 there were six members of the rather unusually named Christmas family living here, with the young Thomas being the 'victualler'.

In 1846 William Honour was in charge but by 1851 his widow, Sarah, was the forty-nine-year-old innkeeper with two teenage nieces, two servants and a lodger. By 1861, The Bell had been taken over by Joseph Norris and his wife Maria, with four children and a niece present. Joseph was originally described as a 'hairdresser' and eventually as a 'licensed victualler' and an innkeeper. The Norris family were resident until the 1880s but by 1891 the publican was thirty-five-year-old John Evans with his wife, Sarah Ann, and four children.

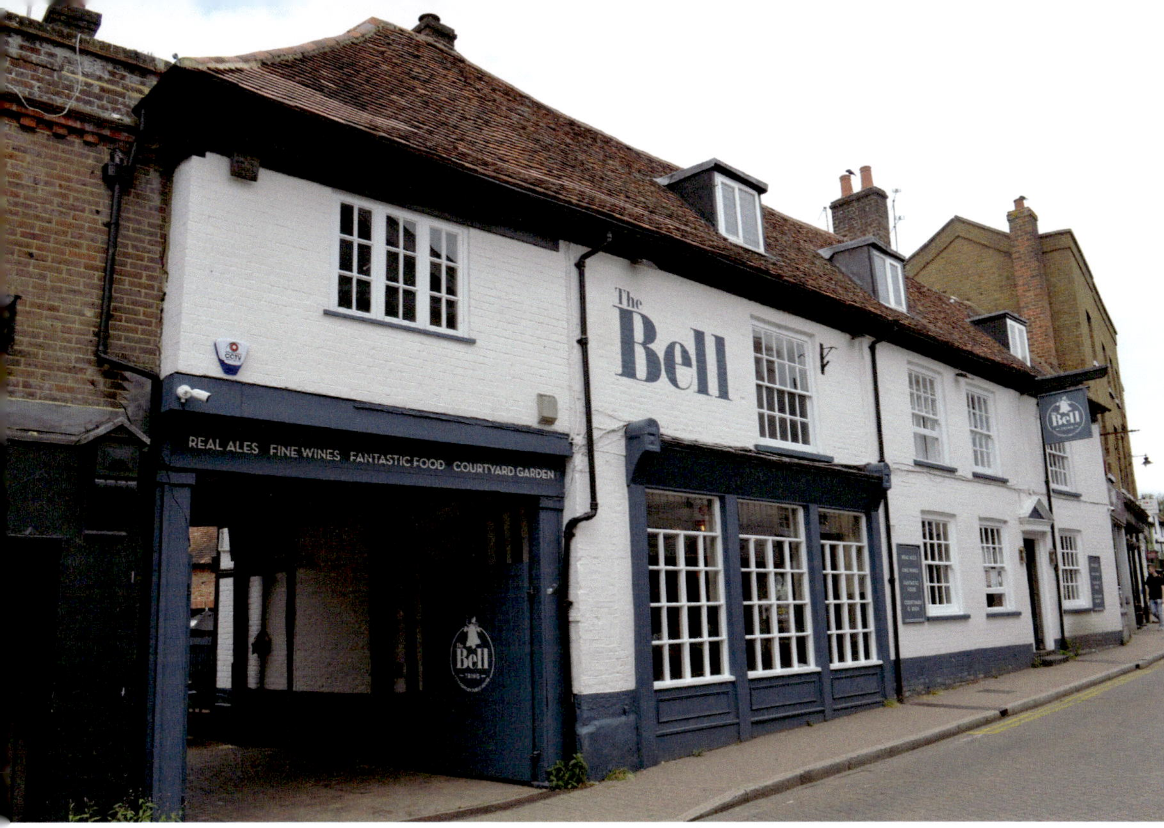

The Bell Inn, in 2015, undergoing renovation in 2023.

By the end of the century, and into the twentieth century, there was a succession of landlords. However, in April 1937 it was decided to convert a number of old buildings at the rear of The Bell into garages. The works revealed some fine old beams which experts thought may date back to the thirteenth century. This building was formerly a coach house for the mail coaches and there were still hayracks and troughs for horses. Whilst the garages are no longer used, the wonderful old beams are still in existence, holding up the roof as they have done for centuries. In March 2023 the pub was leased to Farr Brewery of Wheathampstead and renovation was put in hand.

4. Tring Park and Mansion

Although visually not a part of the town, architectural historian Pevsner describes Tring Park as having 'the appearance of a typical Rothschild mansion.' It is a country house set within Tring Park within the rolling countryside and is now a school for the performing arts, having been a school since the Second World War. It was built in approximately 1682–83 by none other than the architect of St Paul's Cathedral, Sir Christopher Wren, for Henry Guy, who was Secretary of the Treasury to Charles II as well as Groom of the Bedchamber. A later owner was Sir William Gore, who was Lord Mayor of London in 1645 and a founder member of the Bank of England. His son, also William, employed architect James Gibbs in the 1720s. Older views show the old house as a two-storey building of nine bays by seven. It was altered around 1786 for Sir Drummond Smith, a London banker, and eventually purchased in 1872 by Baron Lionel de Rothschild, the first practising Jew to sit as a Member of Parliament, as a wedding present for his son Sir Nathaniel (later Lord) de Rothschild. Like many of the great houses and country seats, over the years, Tring Mansion has been significantly altered externally and especially after 1872 by the Rothschild family. It was partly rebuilt by them but retaining Wren's plan and conception, using red brick with lavish stone dressings and slated Mansard roofs, with the interior extensively refitted in Wren's style. A number of alterations had been carried out by architect George Devey for Lionel Rothschild in 1874; however, the majority of changes were undertaken by William R. Rogers of William Cubitt & Co. after 1879 when Nathaniel inherited the estate.

Now in a French Renaissance style and fashion, the house consists of a basement, two storeys and Mansarded attics, with a near symmetrical entrance front to the north and a similar garden front to the south. The centre of the building has a large stone round-arched *porte cochère* with a balustrade over, with segmental pedimented stone framed dormer windows rising through the parapet.

Tring Park and wandering kangaroos.

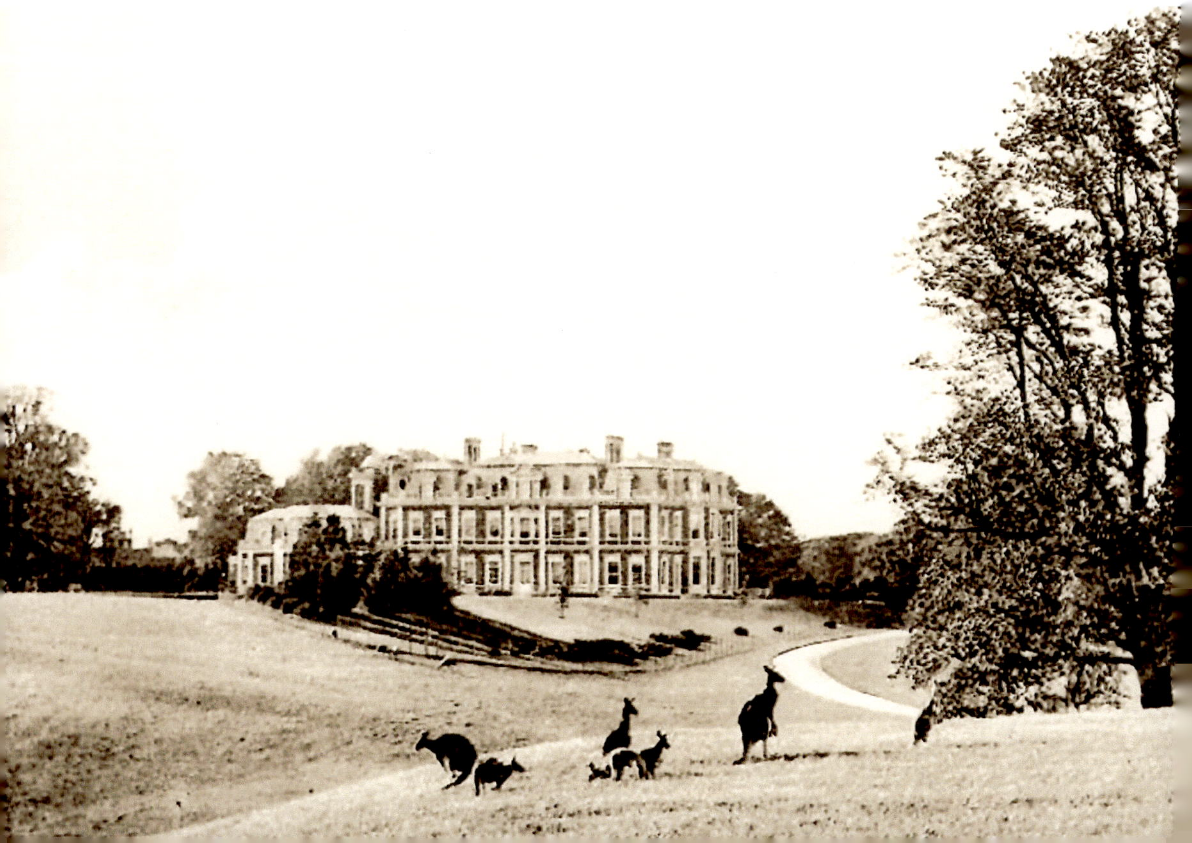

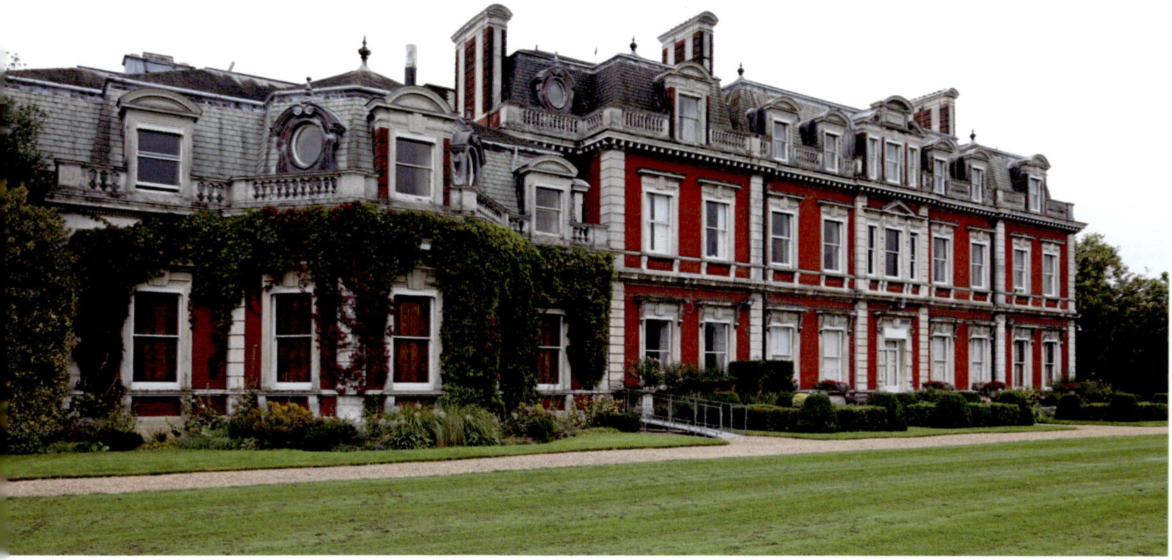

Above: The much-altered Tring Park, in French Renaissance style. (© Peter Jeffree)

Below: Nathaniel Rothschild had the Wren house encased, giving the building you see today. (© Peter Jeffree)

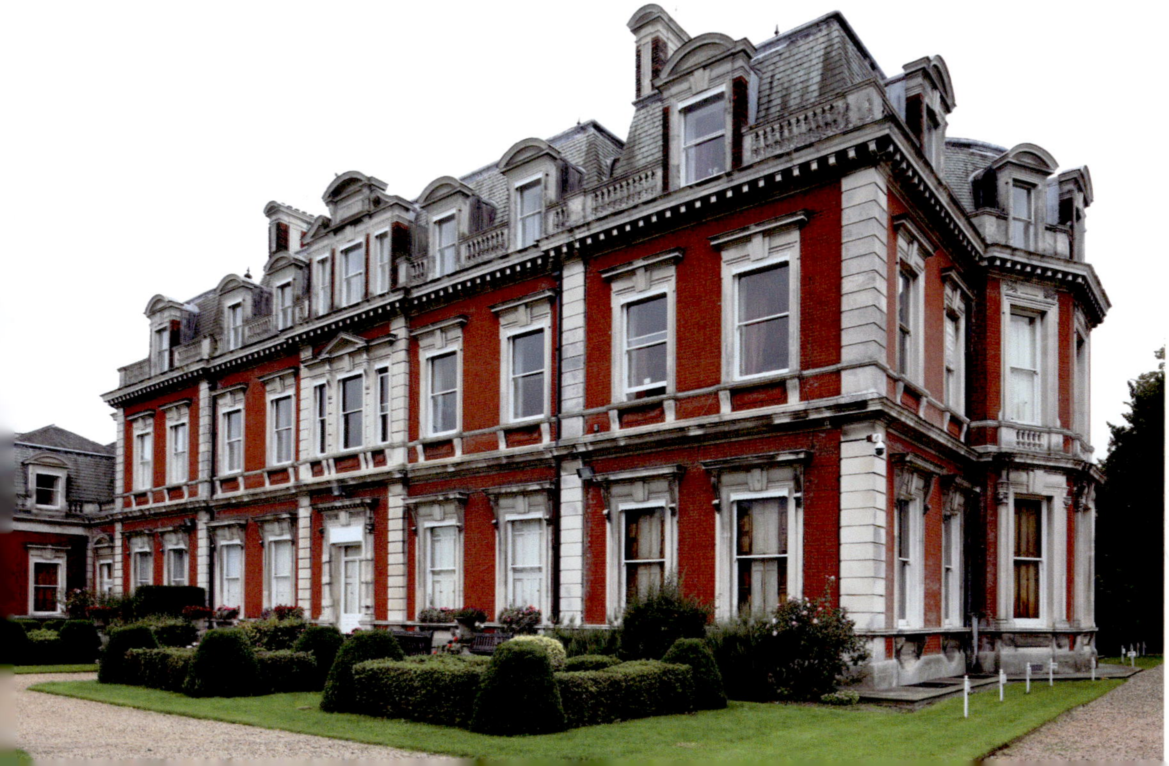

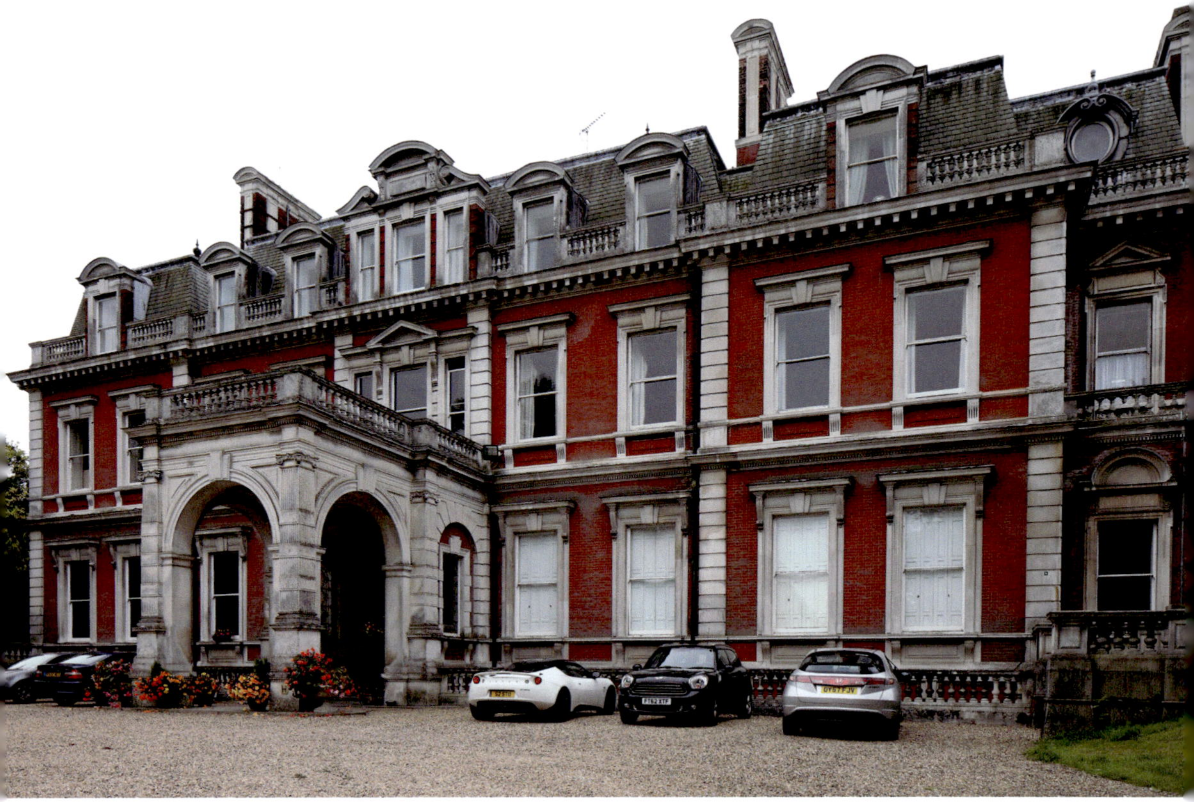

Above: The large stone round-arched *porte cochère* with balustrade above. (© Peter Jeffree)

Below: London Road Lodge, one of a number of lodges to the Tring Park estate.

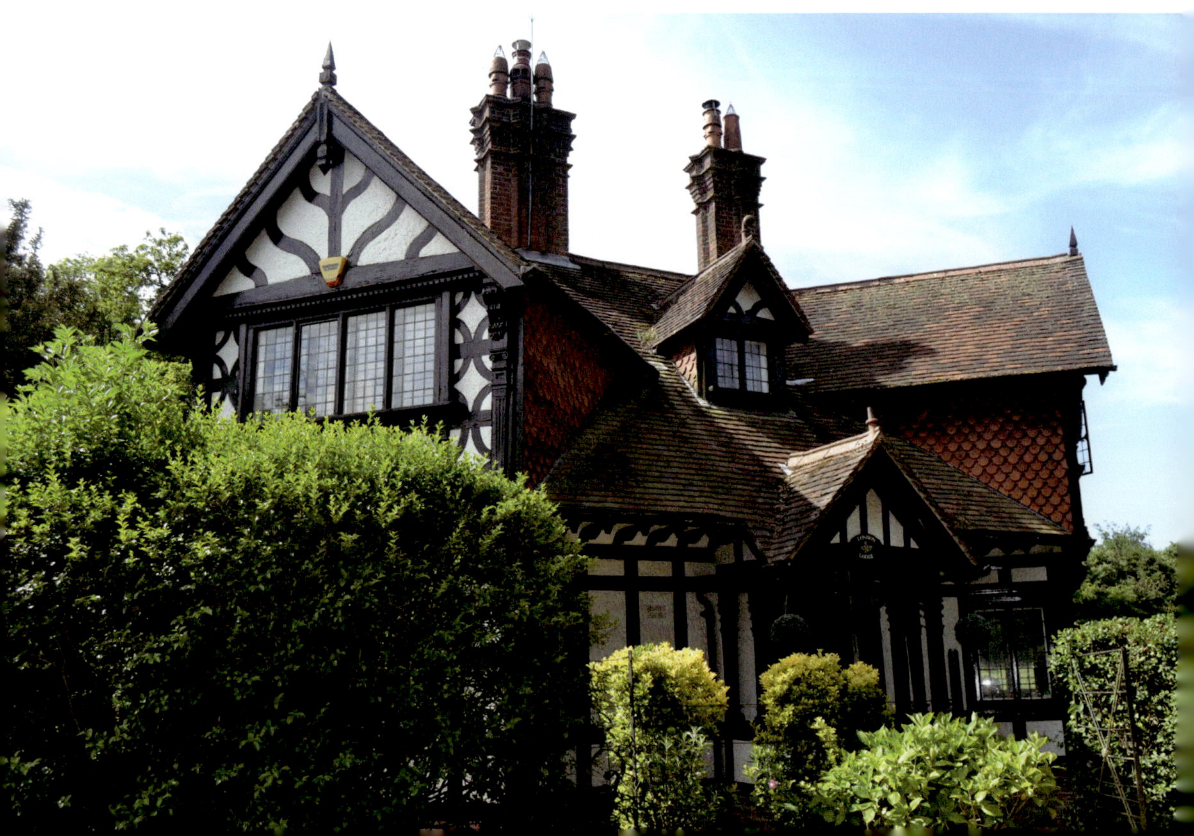

By 1888 Nathaniel Rothschild had encased the Wren house with the house you see today. He doubled the house in size and added another floor. The family had moved out by the start of the Second World War but used the mansion for back-office functions of the Rothschild Bank and as a place of safety for expectant mothers from the east end of London, helped by their Jewish charities. The school arrived in 1945 and has been present ever since.

Tring Park itself is interesting, having been laid out for Sir William Gore by landscape gardener Charles Bridgeman in the 1720s, with a number of buildings by Gibbs, although the landscape is natural in form. Walter Rothschild released cassowaries, kangaroos, zebras, wild horses, tortoises, cranes and emus to roam the park for decades. It was also the venue for the Tring Show, which at one time was the largest one-day agricultural event in the country. Thankfully, Tring Park was saved from becoming a golf course and is now owned by Dacorum Borough Council and leased to the Woodland Trust. At the gateway to the mansion on Park Street are further buildings by Huckvale. This includes the lodge and a number of houses beyond which were built for senior household staff in the 1880s. London Lodge along the London Road marks another entrance to the park.

5. The Robin Hood, Brook Street

Coming into Tring from the western end, one cannot fail to be impressed by Robin Hood, on the corner of Brook Street. It is one of the oldest buildings in Tring, and dates back to the seventeenth century. One of the earliest residents was an elderly widow called Ann Tompkins, who was named as the publican, along with her daughter Elizabeth and son-in-law Henry Beckett, who was to become the licensee. Local press coverage reports of a number of unsavoury incidents in The Robin Hood. The *Bucks Herald* of 26 October 1872 reported 'Elizabeth Lovett, of Tring, was charged by Sergeant Aldridge, with using oaths and profane language at the Robin Hood public house, Tring. She was very abusive, and was brawling about from ten o'clock to one in the morning. She would not be quiet and go home, as he requested her. She said she never saw Sergt. Aldridge at all. She was ordered to pay 14s.6d. fine and costs.'

In 1881, the licensed victualler was Joseph Thornlow from Staffordshire, living with his Boxmoor born wife, Sarah, six cousins, a niece and two visitors. In 1899 the local trade directory listed James Horwood as the licensee and a year later his daughter, Rose, married Thomas James Pearman from Abbots Langley. Thomas was twenty-eight years old in 1901 and it was he who took over as victualler of The Robin Hood with Pearmans present for most of the twentieth century. Thomas was well known locally as a keen photographer and had a studio at the rear of the pub. Many of his photographs still remain. Thomas sadly died at the age of fifty-nine years old after spending fourteen

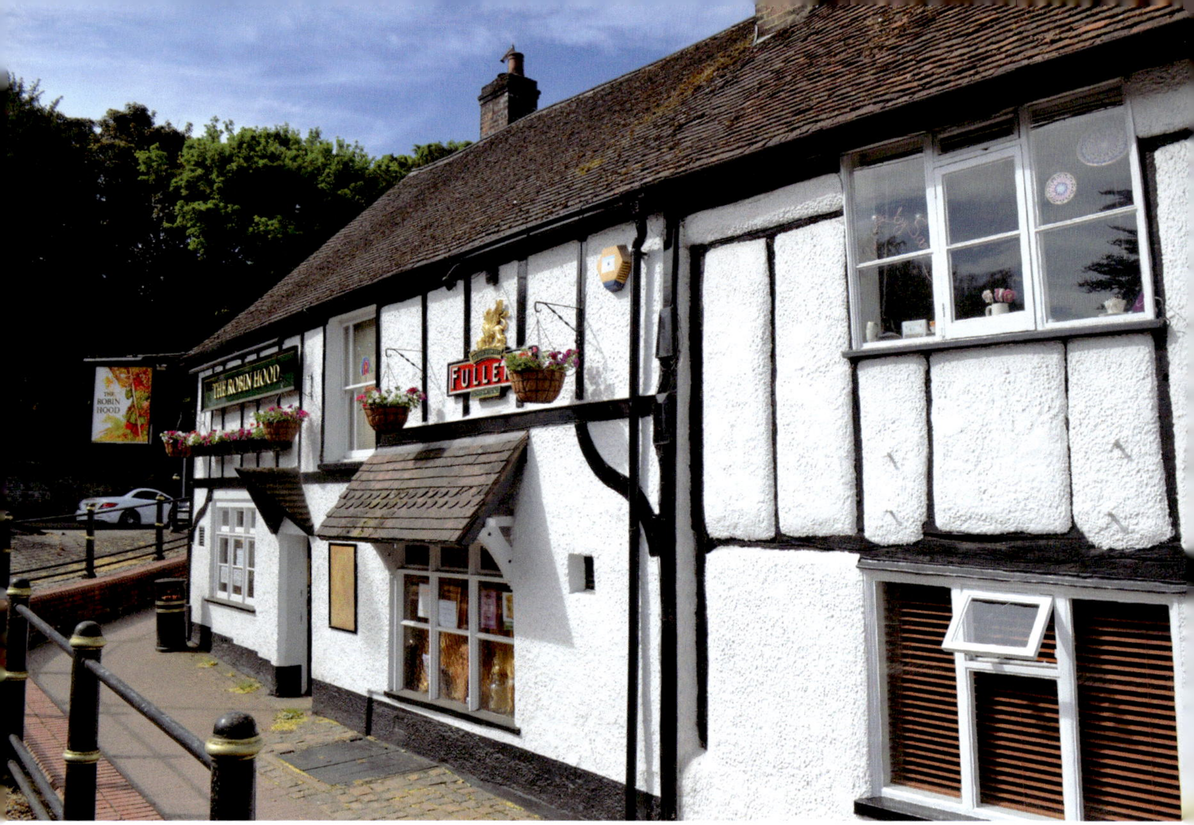

The Robin Hood, one of the oldest, yet prominent buildings in Tring and occasionally visited by Hollywood film stars.

weeks in the West Herts Hospital, with the business carried on by his second wife and one son.

As with many of Tring's remaining public houses, it remains popular and hit the local news in 2023 when Hollywood star Keanu Reeves recently visited it whilst in the area.

6. The Former Plough Inn, No. 50 High Street

This is one of the oldest buildings in Tring and has changed very little over many decades. The Friendly Society held meetings here in 1794 when it was already called The Plough Inn. Many meetings were held here for a wide range of local societies holding their annual dinners, with a large room at the back accommodating a large number of people. The rifle club was another user, with very few buildings having space for such an activity. From 1861, many publicans were residents but by 27 July 1878, John Penn was the host. In 1905, The Plough was transferred to the Herts Public House Trust Co. Ltd, which had the Rose and Crown, and The Plough was used as a booking office for the hotel. It was eventually purchased by Mr John Bly, Snr, for his antique business. When he died in 1937 it was carried on by his son, Frank, and then Frank's son, John. He eventually transferred his business

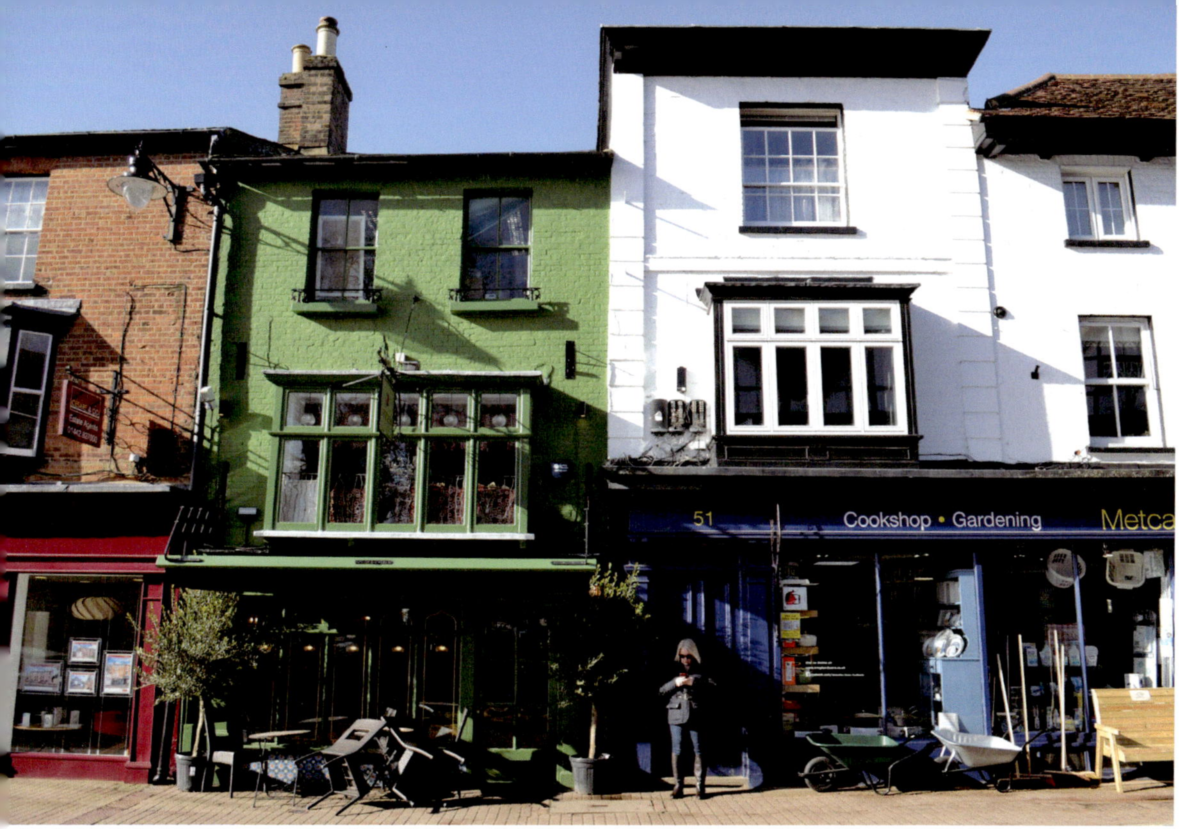

The former Plough Inn with adjacent properties with historical connections.

to London and the property became New England House Antiques, followed by a vegetarian restaurant and coffee shop, and it has remained a restaurant since then. Next door premises at Nos 51–52 were commandeered by the Royal Navy in 1940 as HMS Aeolus, making kites and balloons for the war effort.

7. Grace's Maltings, Akeman Street

One could almost miss Grace's Maltings, almost hidden and out of the way off Akeman Street. Today, what remains has been converted into residential properties. The former entrance to the maltings was off Akeman Street to what was a malting and mill, which dated from medieval times right up until the First World War. After the war, it was run as a corn mill for another fifty years and took its name from Frank Grace and his sons Thomas and Robert, who ran it later. By the 1980s, the mill had ceased operation and had been bought by property developers, who converted many of the buildings and surrounding area into private dwellings, but sadly only retaining some of the original building's characteristics.

The former Grace's Maltings is much altered, but does include the remnants of the early sixteenth-century hall house of cruck construction, floored in the seventeenth century. It also has a north cross-wing with kiln, maltings, and grain store.

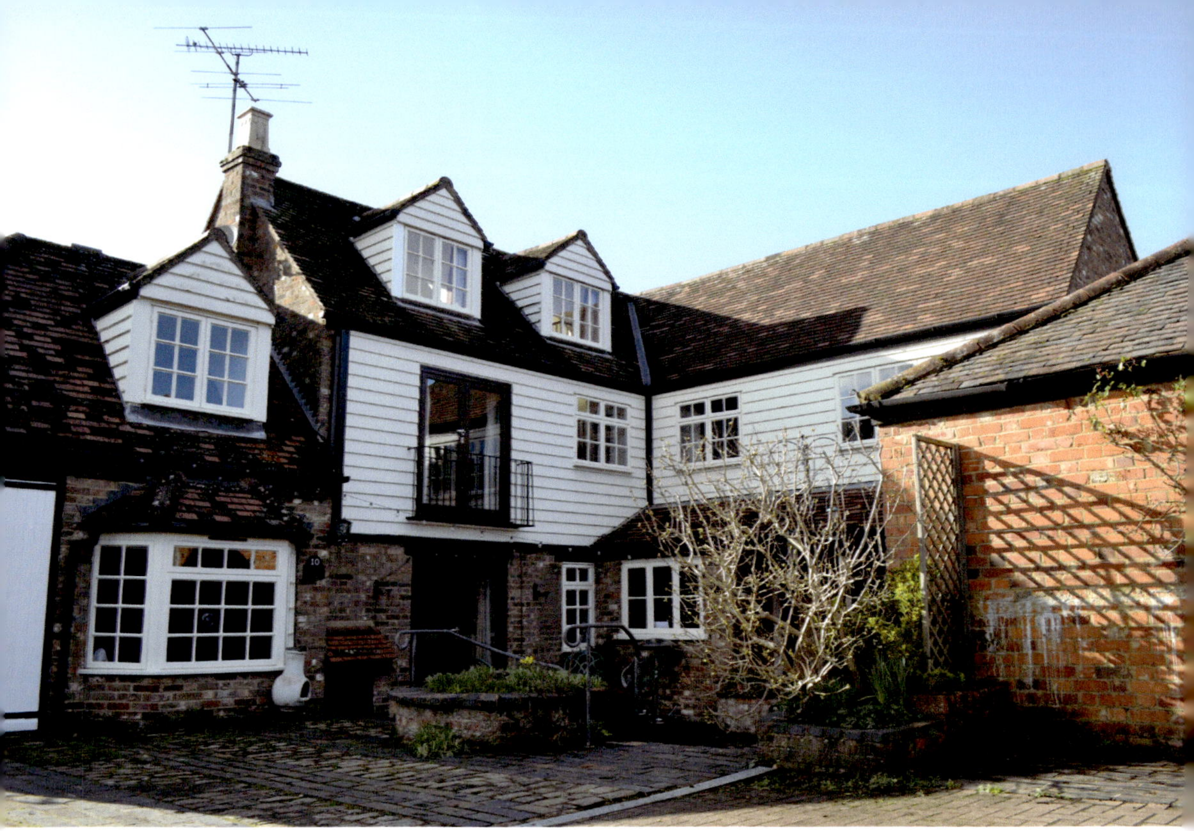

Above: The former Grace's Maltings, now residential.

Below: An example of restoration and preservation.

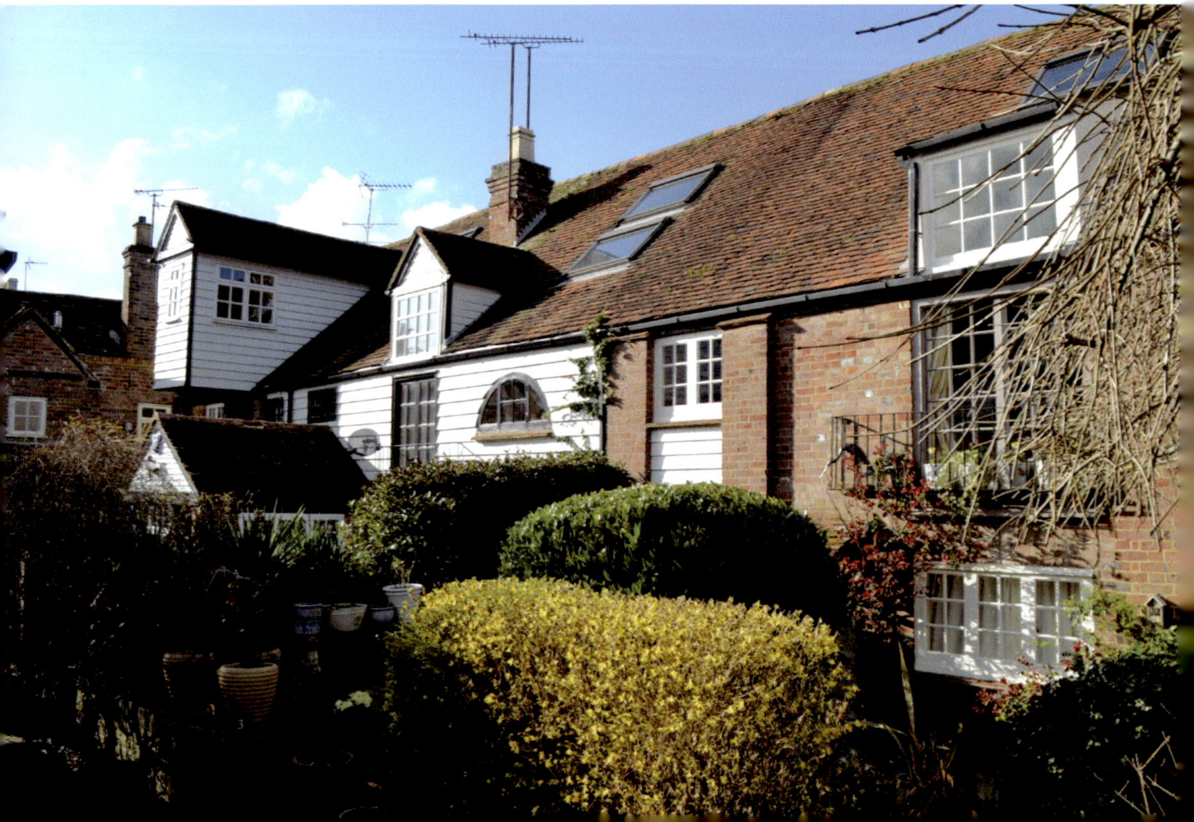

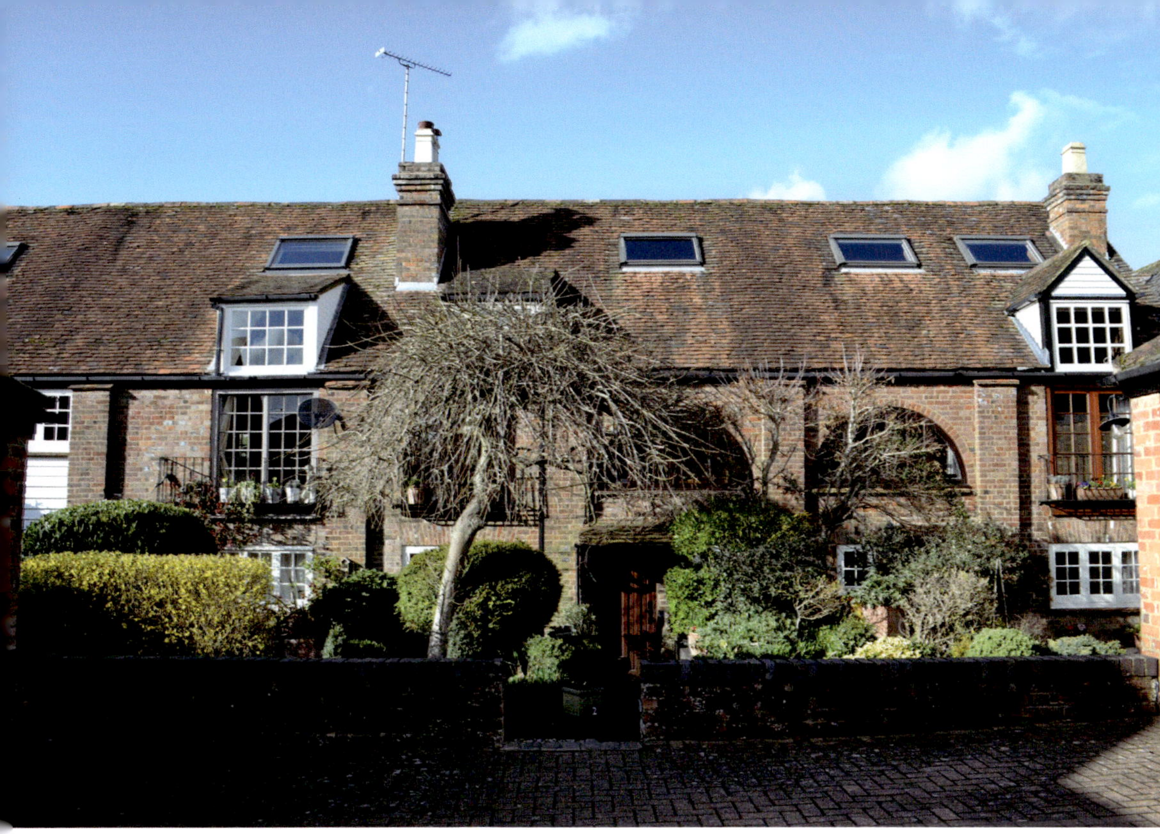

Hidden away off Akeman Street, but part of Tring's history.

To the east side south of Grace's Maltings are early nineteenth-century cottages little altered. The east side continues south with cottages mostly dating from *c.* 1800. Few are of great interest individually, but collectively they reflect Tring's history of early nineteenth-century industry and commerce. No. 20, a modern building on the corner of Rodwell Yard, has a timber frame in its side wall, a strange relic of an earlier structure. Behind is the vast maltings, now converted to residential use, built by John Brown, the brewer, of No. 24 High Street.

8. The Former George Public House, Frogmore Street

The original George public house was not on the corner of the High Street but in Frogmore Street, beyond a shop that stood on the corner. In 1806, it was described as 'a small hostelry and corn chandler' held by Mr Joseph Tompkins. In 1830 the publican was William Clarke, and by 1870 it was George Sills.

A new building of the George Hotel was planned on the corner of the High Street as reported in the *Bucks Herald* on 13 February 1897. It said: 'The Aylesbury Brewery Company will move the new George Building 7ft 6in higher up from Frogmore Street and fill in the cellar at a cost of £150.' By late summer, the building was under construction. It was not the only time that the George was to feature in the local newspapers. In 1900, the new licensee that had taken over from Mr John Saunders,

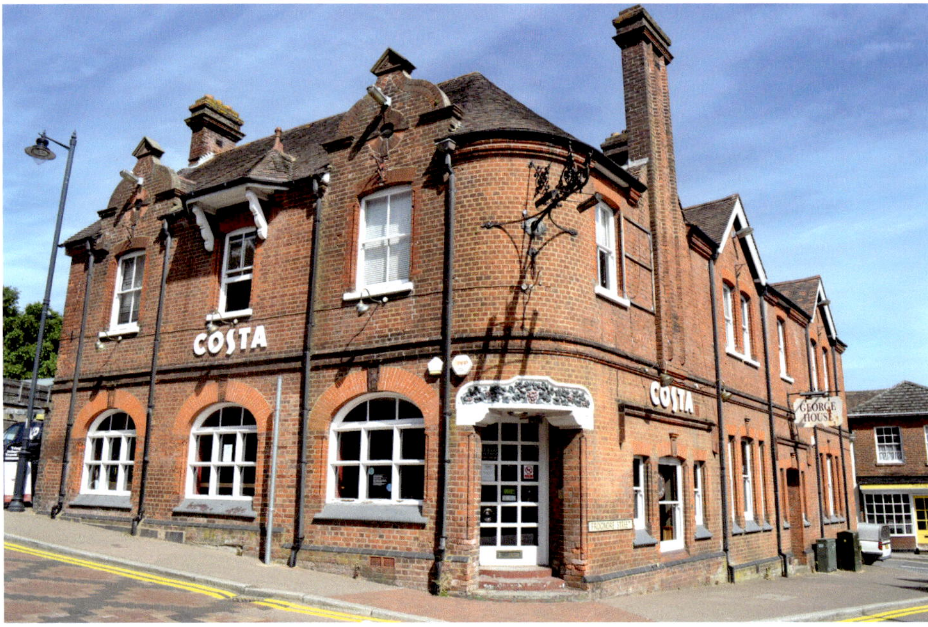

Once a popular hotel in Tring, the George has succumbed to the Costa Coffee global empire.

who had died suddenly of an apoplectic fit, had an issue with one of his customers. On 17 March, the paper reported: 'An elderly man received serious injuries while being forcibly removed from the George Hotel. He cut his head and face severely. Several versions of the affair are in circulation.' The headline the following week read, 'Pushing an old man down the George steps.' The licensee Alfred Horwood was charged with assaulting and beating the old man at Berkhamsted Petty Sessions, but the magistrates dismissed the case, clearly of the view the 'assault' was justified.

The George Hotel was in business for many years and was an important building on the busy High Street. By the 1980s, though, it housed the John Harvey Collection, a mail-order clothing company. Following that, it became an estate agents called Cole, Flatt and Partners, who retained the old name of the building by calling it George House. Today it is home to Costa Coffee.

9. New Mill Baptist Church

The Baptist Church at New Mill is one of the oldest in Hertfordshire, established in the period of religious liberty that prevailed between the Civil War and the restoration of the monarchy. The present church and Sunday school buildings were built in 1818 and 1897, respectively, but the history of Baptists at New Mill goes back to the time of Oliver Cromwell. In, or about, the year 1655, six persons formed themselves into a Baptist Church. Their first place of worship was a mud-walled cottage which stood close to the site of the present building.

In 1666 the Five-Mile Act came into force, forbidding any Nonconformist minister from being within 5 miles of any place where they had been ministers. Records state that 'the little church at New Mill had to leave their retired meeting-house, and go into the woods to worship God, for fear of their persecutors.' Their night-time meeting place was discovered and the pastor Richard Sutton was arrested and sent to prison, where he remained until the death of Charles II. A local official is reputed to have said 'Sutton, you have preached a good sermon and now you must suffer for it.' With the accession of James II, legal changes to allow Roman Catholic worship also granted religious liberty to Nonconformist churches. Richard Sutton was freed and New Mill chapel was reopened; around this time John Bunyan is reputed to have visited and preached on several occasions.

Despite being granted freedom to worship, Baptists were a despised set of people and the New Mill meeting was small with a membership of fewer than twenty. No new minister was appointed and for a number of years the church appears to have been closed, its remaining members worshipping at Dunstable. It was during John Clement's ministry that a baptistry was installed. In the first volume of the *Baptist Magazine* for 1809 we are told that during his ministry, 'the meeting has been several times enlarged; and they have erected a new stable and cart-house, sufficiently roomy to receive twenty horses and ten to twelve carts and chaises, so many being employed to convey the worshippers to the place. They dine in the vestry room, and have from one to two hundred at the prayer-meeting after dinner.'

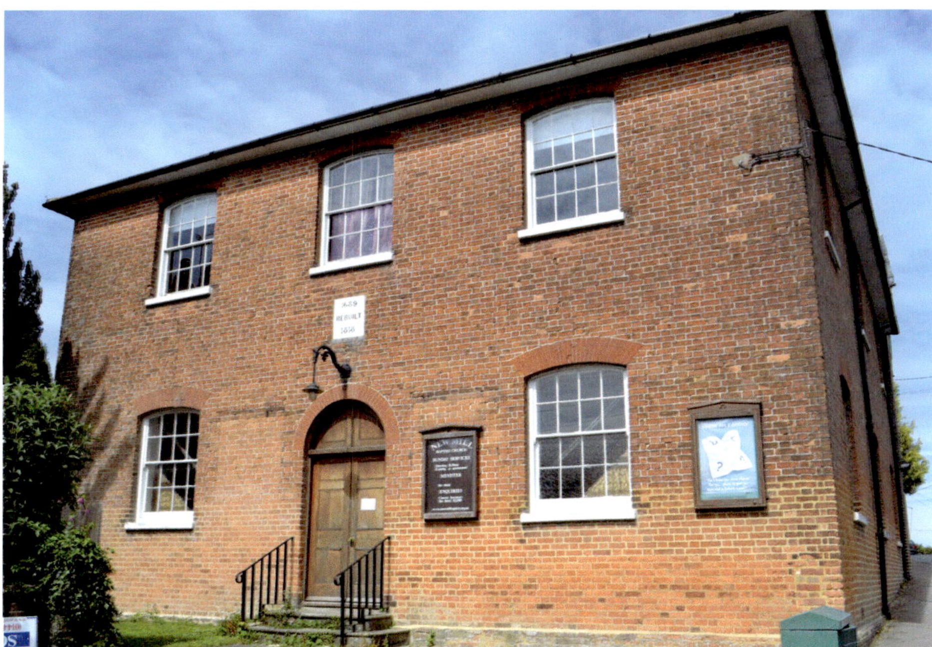

New Mill Baptist Church.

In January 1817 Daniel Clarabut, the schoolmaster, was ordained pastor. It was during the early part of his ministry that the present chapel was erected and regularly filled with 'attentive hearers'. The villages around were constantly visited, not only by the pastor but by various lay helpers. The church grew and by 1827 church membership stood at 212. Daniel Clarabut died in 1833 aged forty-one. In December 1853, the police had to be summoned to help control a crowded church meeting and at a further meeting were asked to prevent some of the deacons from entering the church.

In October 1874, Revd W. V. Young became the pastor. Ill health caused him to retire from this post in March 1882. During his ministry, half an acre of land was donated to the church by Sir Nathaniel de Rothschild in order to enlarge the burial ground. The whole of the land was then walled in, planted, laid out and new iron gates erected.

For many years morning and afternoon services had been held at New Mill, and evening services at the Tabernacle in Akeman Street, but the increasing population of New Mill and the gift of the manse (in Grove Road), led to the evening services transferring to New Mill. In 1890 the Sunday school at New Mill numbered

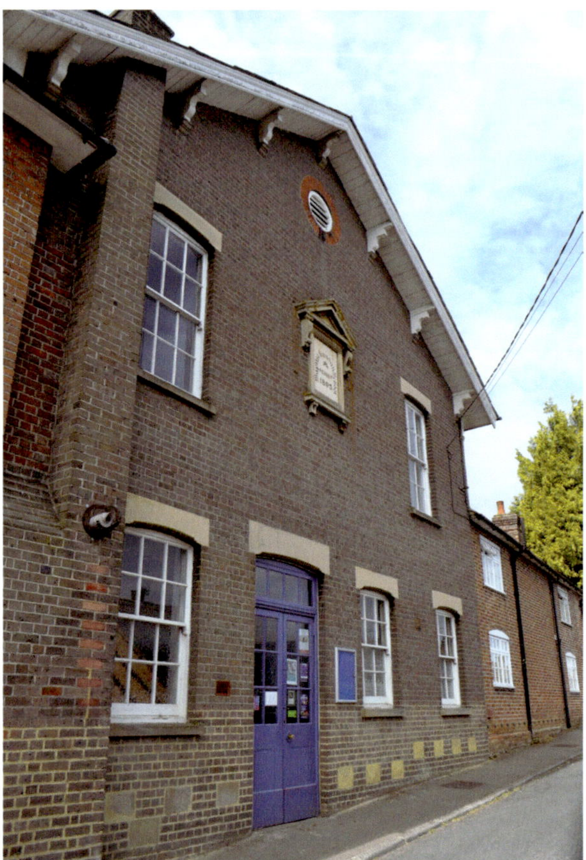

The Sunday school, which opened in 1895.

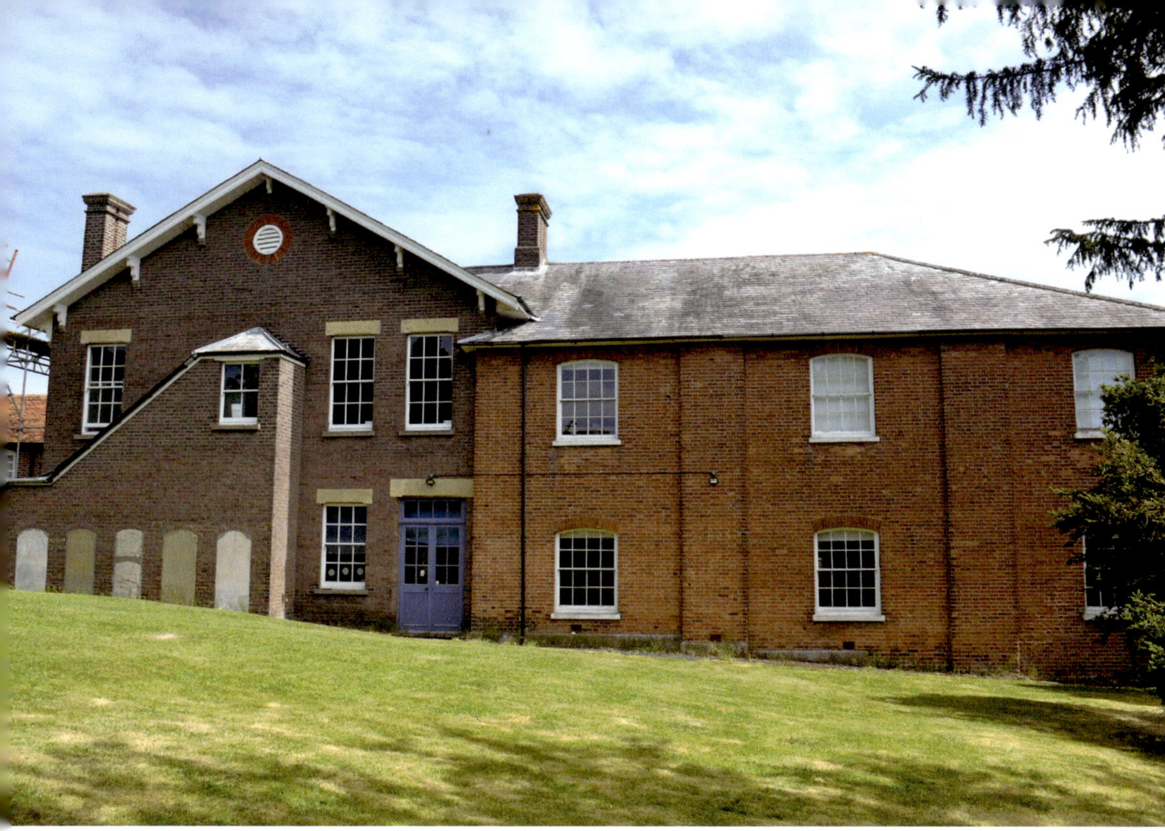

New Mill Sunday School and Baptist Chapel.

350 scholars and forty teachers. In 1895 soon after Revd H. J. Martin became pastor, a new road from Wingrave Road to the schoolroom was built. Plans were laid for the building of the present schoolroom and the building was completed and opened in 1897 at a cost of £1,015.05.

In 1952, a formal notice was received from the Ministry of Local Government and Planning that the new Mill Baptist Church has been scheduled as a Building of Historic Interest.

10. The Old Vicarage and Gatehouse

The date of Tring's old vicarage has stirred debate for many years including when it was described as a 'former vicarage … picturesque gabled Tudor of 1828, with a fine collection of decorative chimneys (which were specially designed for Charles Lacy, the incumbent) with additions in 1873'. It is likely to have been built by the Rev. Lacy in 1825. It proved expensive and too large to maintain and in 1920 the vicar, Revd T. V. Garnier, moved to a smaller house. It eventually became the residence of the well-known cricketer Mr Kemp, who was also Harrow master.

The house was given new life as Sutton Court, renovated and converted into offices by Melvin, Lansley & Mark, between 1971 and 1975. A new office wing was added, and next to it a bold and attractive parish hall with sharply angled roofs.

By the churchyard is a very pretty neo-Tudor brick and stone gatehouse, which is of interest as many local residents perceive this as being the original building. In 1972, it was in a very poor condition and was reported in the *Bucks Herald* in August under the headline 'Controversial Tring Victorian Gatehouse'. It stated

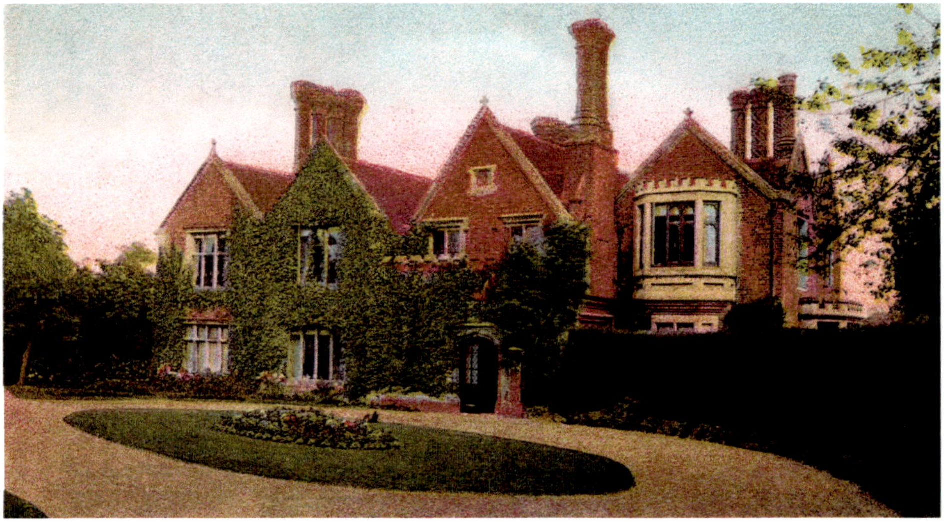

Above: An early view of the former vicarage.

Below: The former vicarage today.

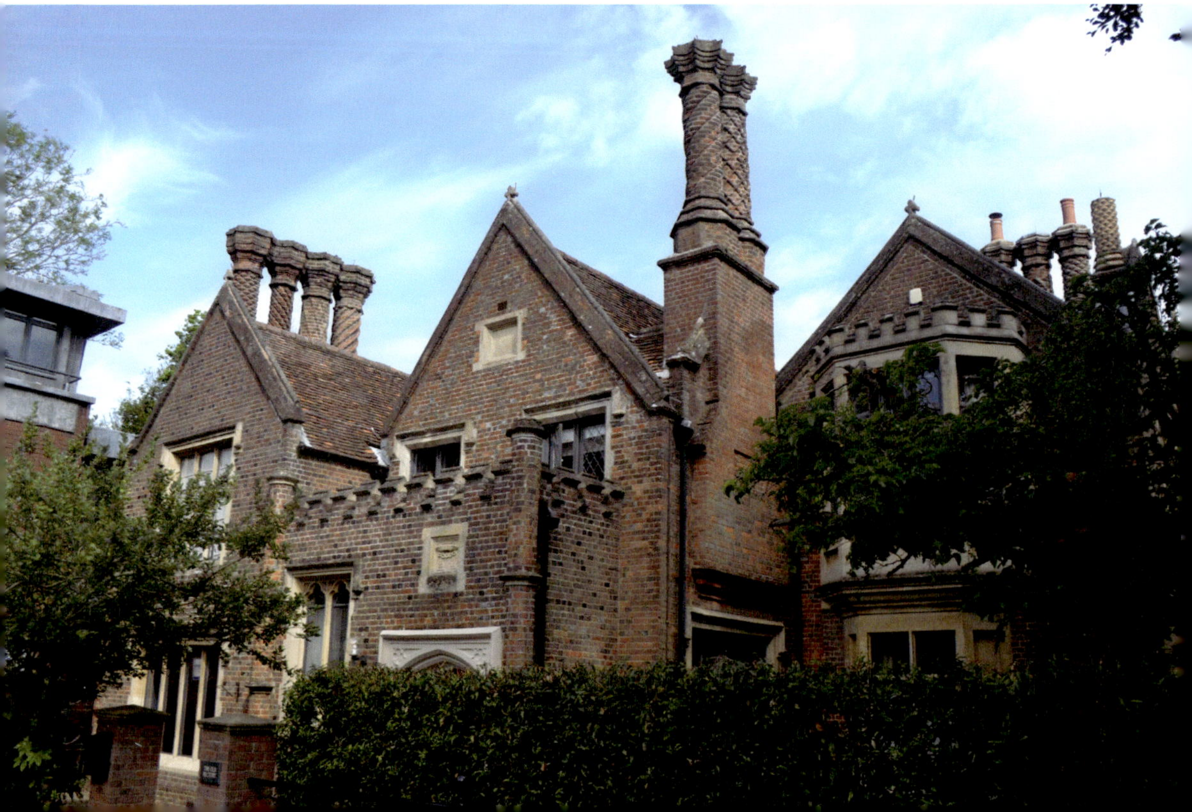

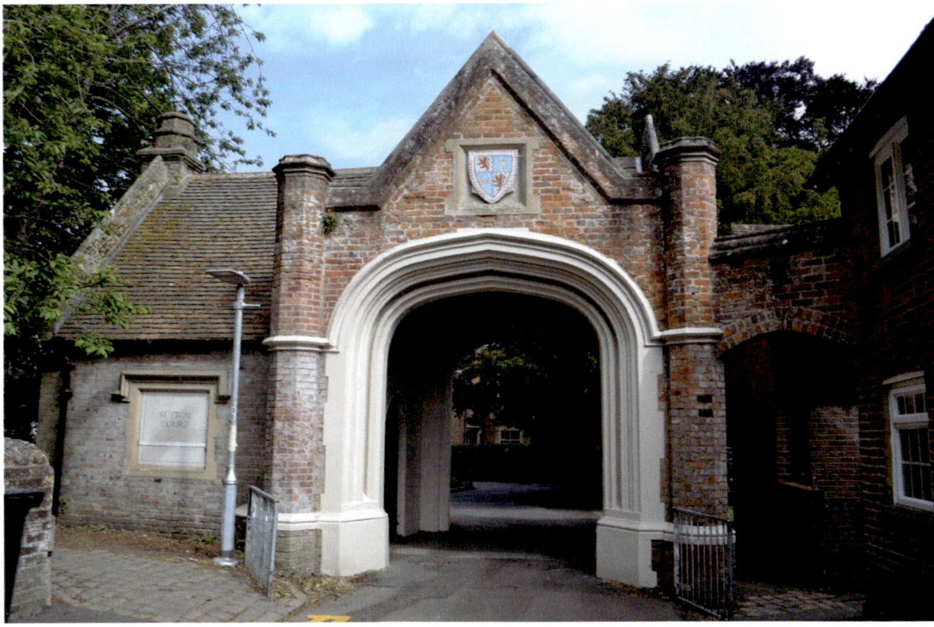

Original or recreation of the original – the gatehouse into the former vicarage.

'Planning permission has been given for the gatehouse of the Old Vicarage, constructed in early Victorian times, to be demolished and reinstated in matching design. A new vicarage has been built and the old vicarage is to be used for offices. The future of the picturesque gatehouse caused some controversy in the town, resulting in the decision to demolish it because of the crumbling state, and then to reinstate it because of the character it gives to the town centre.' It was eventually dismantled and is a fine example of a recreated building.

11. Former Brown's Brewery

There appears to have been a brewery at No. 24 High Street since the very early part of the nineteenth century. The earliest known owner was Thomas Amsden, who has been described as a common brewer and also owned the White Lion at Aston Clinton. James Field was the next owner of this brewery in *c.* 1826 and then passed to John Brown under whose ownership it remained for many decades.

John Brown was born on New Year's Eve 1795 in Okeford Fitzpaine in Dorset and moved to Tring in 1826, where he established his brewery and built several public houses in the area. In the 1830s, the London & Birmingham Railway line was built, which passed near the town. The navvies employed in its construction provided much of the business for breweries in Tring, including that of John Brown.

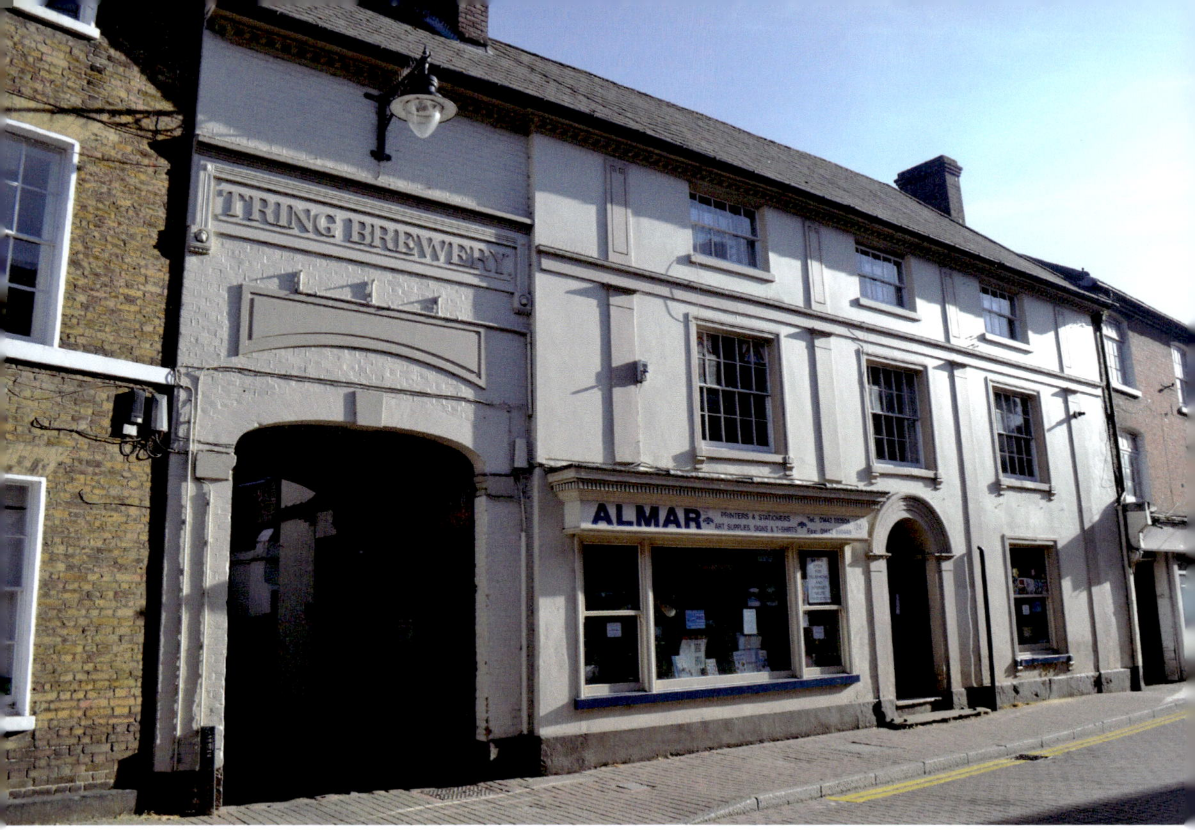

Above: Brewing in Tring has always been an institution.

Below: Former brewery buildings, visible from the High Street.

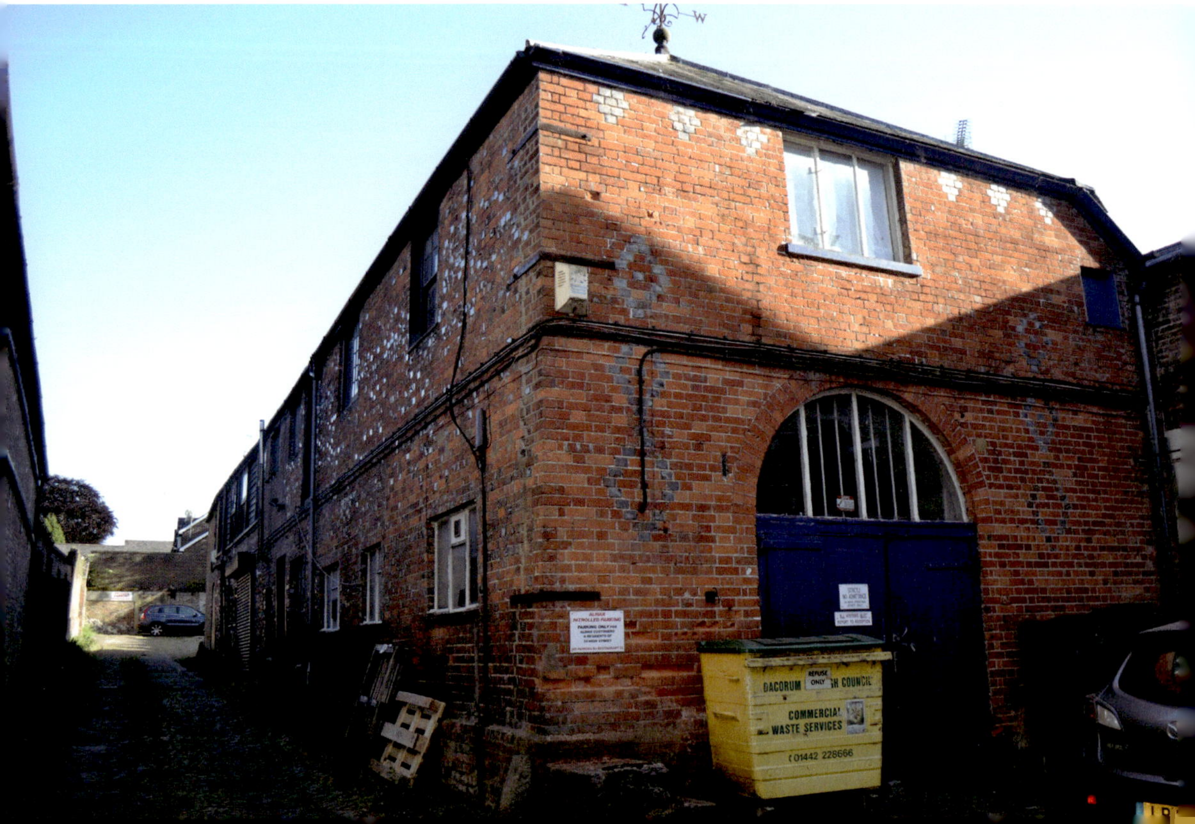

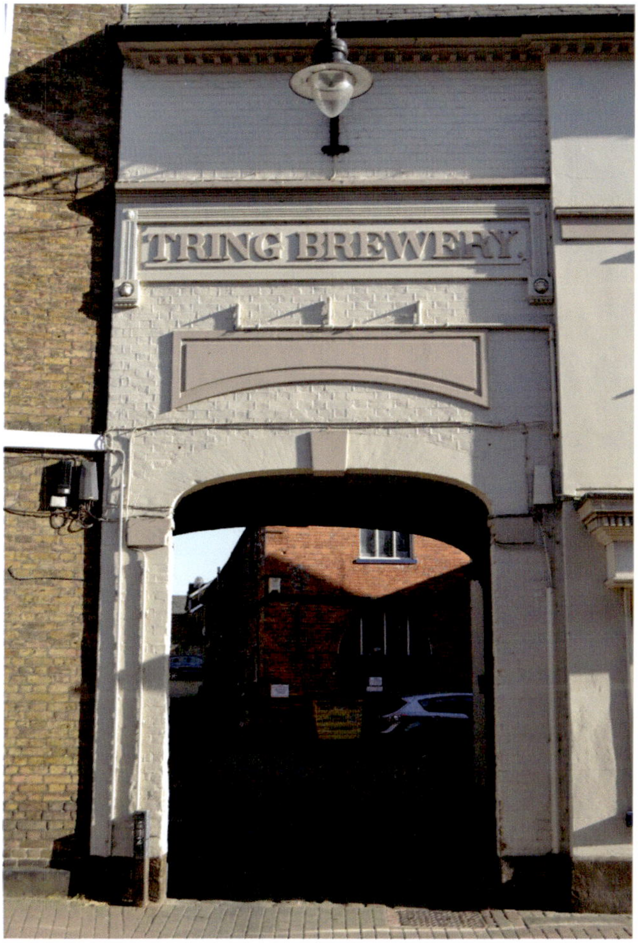

A peep into Tring's brewing past.

During the 1830s he built several pubs in the area, which had a distinctive architectural style. In Tring, these included the Britannia (now Norfolk House) and the King's Arms. The *Bucks Herald* was advertising in December 1836, 'Public Houses Wanted, Wanted to Rent or Purchase, a Compact Road-side Public House, with a small quantity of Land attached. Also to Rent, two respectable Public Houses in a Market town in Herts or Bucks. Coming in not exceeding 500l. Apply (if by letter, post-paid) to Mr. W. Brown, Auctioneer, Tring.'

In 1851 John was a farmer and a wine and spirit merchant, as well as a brewer; in 1881 he was employing nine men at the brewery. In later years the brewery was run by John's son John Herbert Brown; he and his brother Frederick William took over when John died in 1890. However, John Herbert died in 1896, and in 1898 Frederick William sold the brewery, with nine freehold public houses, to Locke and Smith of Berkhamsted.

Brown's distinctive architectural style was used in a number of pubs in and around Tring as he expanded his estate. Many are included in this book.

12. King's Arms Public House

The King's Arms was built in the early nineteenth century around 1830, for John Brown's Tring Brewery. When it was built, the pub's land included the far end of Charles Street and the pub's orchard was where the two bungalows 'Cosy Corner' and 'Corners' now stand. The 'KA', as it is known by regulars, has always been a pub, and internally the layout has changed very little. Brown built grandly beside what was then the main London to Aylesbury road with the expectation that expansion of the town would follow its completion. Unfortunately, the expected growth failed to materialise and the town centre expanded slowly elsewhere, taking the main road along what became Western Road and the High Street. This left the pub somewhat isolated; it later became surrounded by houses, shops and workshops that is now known as the 'Tring Triangle'. At some time during the second half of the nineteenth century the range of stables and warehousing that bound the garden were built, one assumes by the brewery for general commercial use. In 1897, the Ancient Order of Foresters celebrated their fifteenth anniversary in the Court Room at the Kings Arms. It was a grand occasion with members of the order marching in procession to the parish church, led by the Tring Brass band.

The colourful King's Arms.

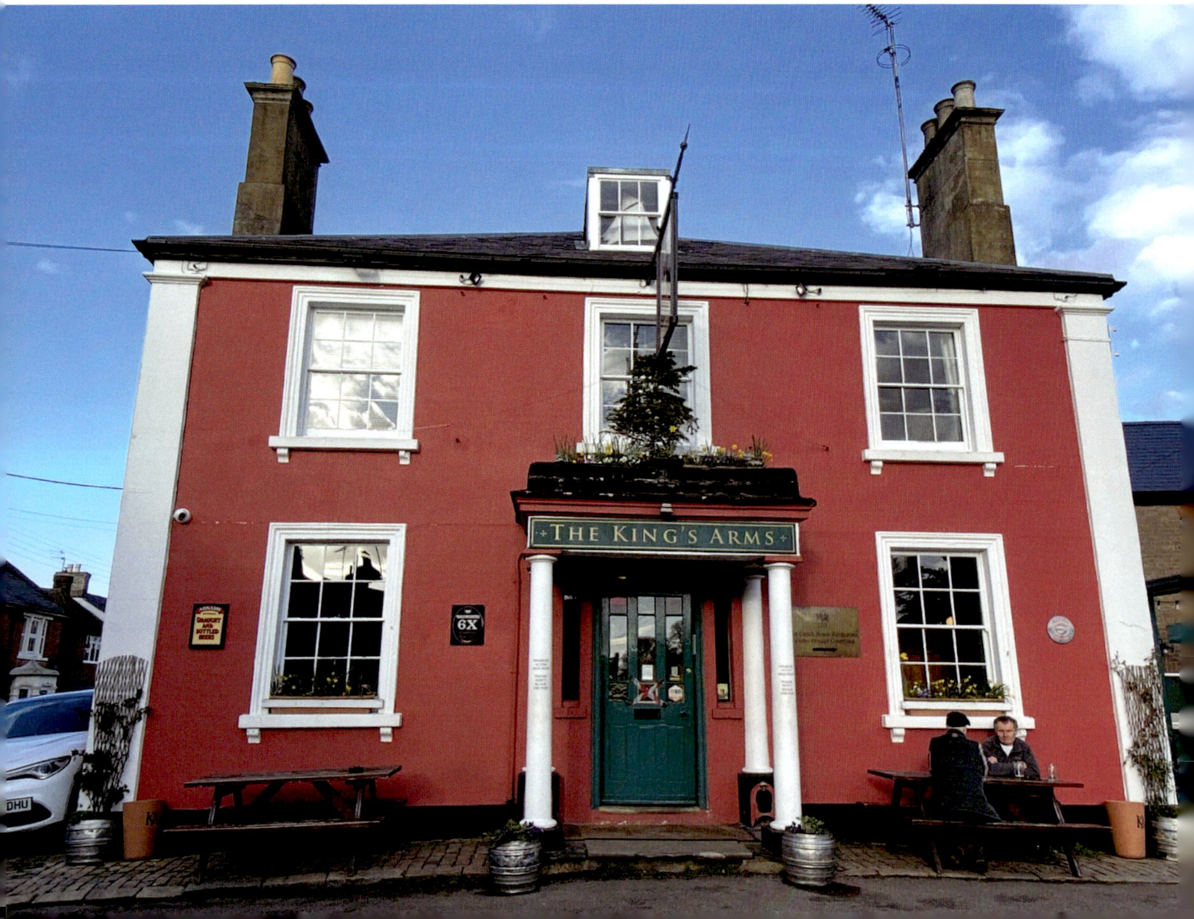

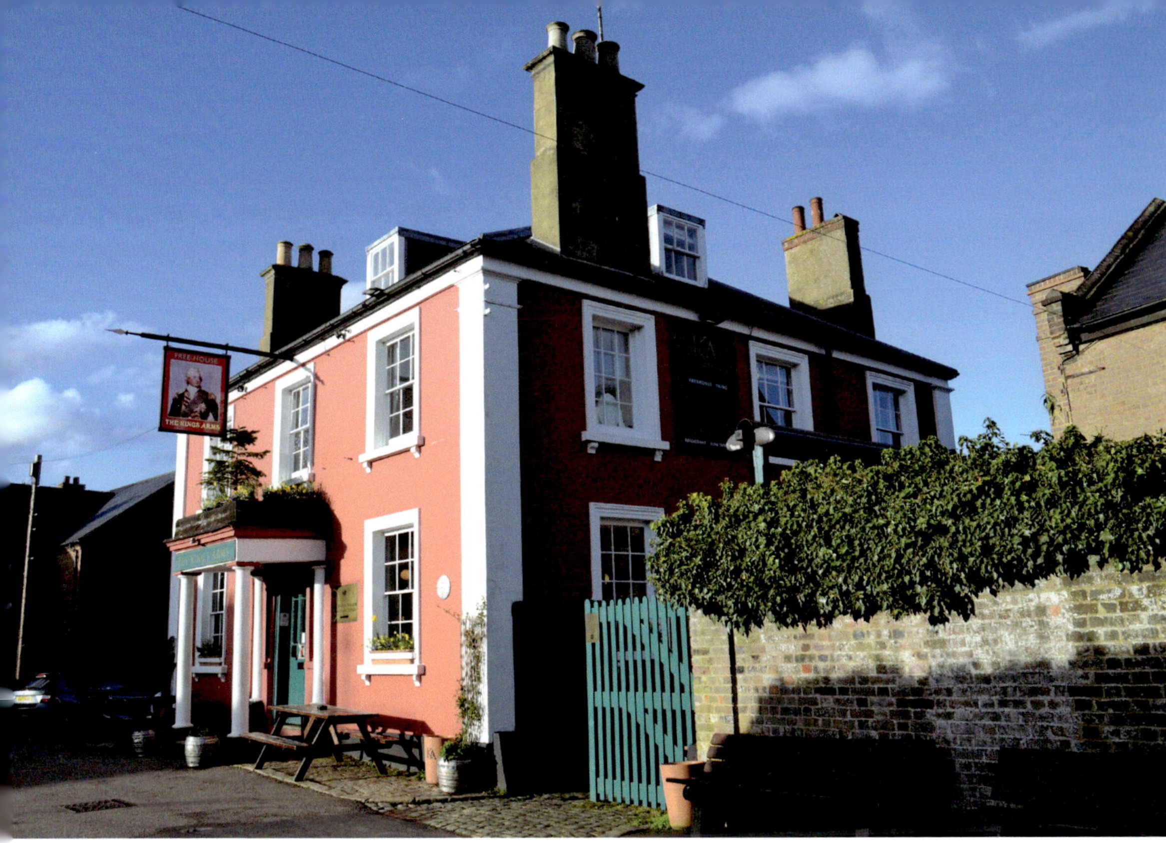

Above: Fondly known today as the KA.

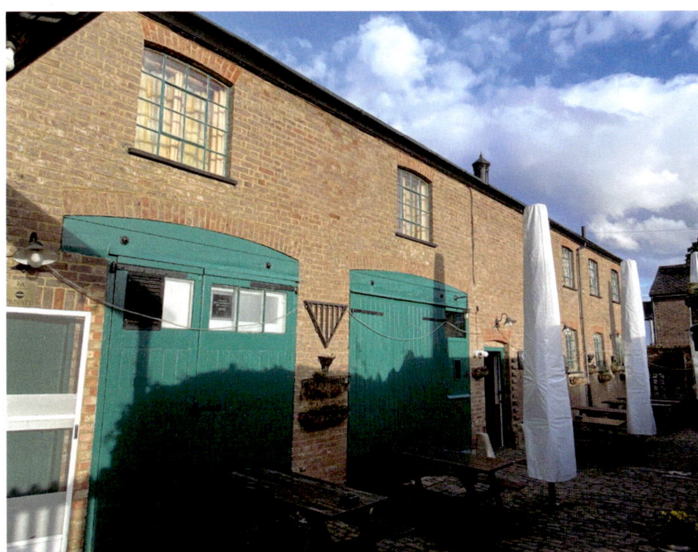

Right: To the rear are the range of stables and warehousing.

In 1898 Brown's pubs were bought by Locke and Smith's Berkhamsted Brewery, which in turn went to Benskin's Watford Brewery in 1913. Author and novelist Graham Greene records in his novel *A Sort of Life*, as a young man in Berkhamsted around 1920, taking 'exciting car rides to the King's Arms in the neighbouring town of Tring'.

In 1957 Benskin's in turn was taken over by Ind Coope as part of what became a geographical domination of pub possession by the notorious 'Big Six' brewers. In the hands of Allied Breweries many pubs suffered incomprehensible neglect and asset stripping through the 1970s. The King's Arms orchard was sold off in the late 1960s and the warehouse buildings were let to a maker of sweets, pickles and jam. The KA (along with a number of other local pubs) was closed, boarded up and offered for sale in 1979.

It was not expected that any of these pubs would reopen; one that did was the King's Arms. In June 1981 it eventually reopened. The pink, grey and green colour scheme was chosen to distance the pub from previous corporate brewery colours and customary drab, cream nicotine-stained interiors associated with many earlier pubs. It remains a popular community pub in Tring.

13. Baptist Chapel, Akeman Street

Baptist Nonconformity had been established in England in 1607 when John Smyth, an ordained Anglican minister, separated from the Church of England and introduced the Baptism of adult believers as the foundation of church membership. Tring is notable for the strength of its Baptist tradition and the consequent number of Baptist chapels. The first indication of dissent in the town was in 1662 when fifty-two Quakers and Baptists were prosecuted for offences of nonconformity. The period of the greatest expansion for Nonconformist denominations was from the mid-eighteenth century up to about 1870, as non-Anglican worshippers were gradually freed from constraints on their civil liberties. Around 1715 a survey records sixty-two Baptist families in Tring, and by the 1880s there were five Baptist chapels that accommodated around 500 members with 800 children – a significant proportion of the town's population of about 3,500. The chapel in Akeman Street was the fourth to be established. Its origins date to 1801 when dissatisfied members from two other chapels joined together to worship in a barn in Frogmore End. In 1808 they built a new meeting house in Akeman Street, and their pastor Richard Glover was so successful that in 1832 the current chapel was built, seating 850 members. The 1887 Ordnance Survey map shows that there was a burial ground occupying the long plot to the west of the chapel, an area now consisting of a lawn. The grave monuments are now located in a small area at the western end. There are two Grade II listed obelisks in front of the chapel in memory of previous pastors: the south one, dating to *c.* 1851, is in memory of James Page; and the north one, dating to *c.* 1861, is in memory of Richard Glover.

The building has been subject to alterations and extensions. The seating on the ground floor of the chapel is not original; the precise date when it was replaced is unknown but it was probably in the third quarter of the nineteenth century. Between 1897 and 1898 the two-storey rear extension was added to provide

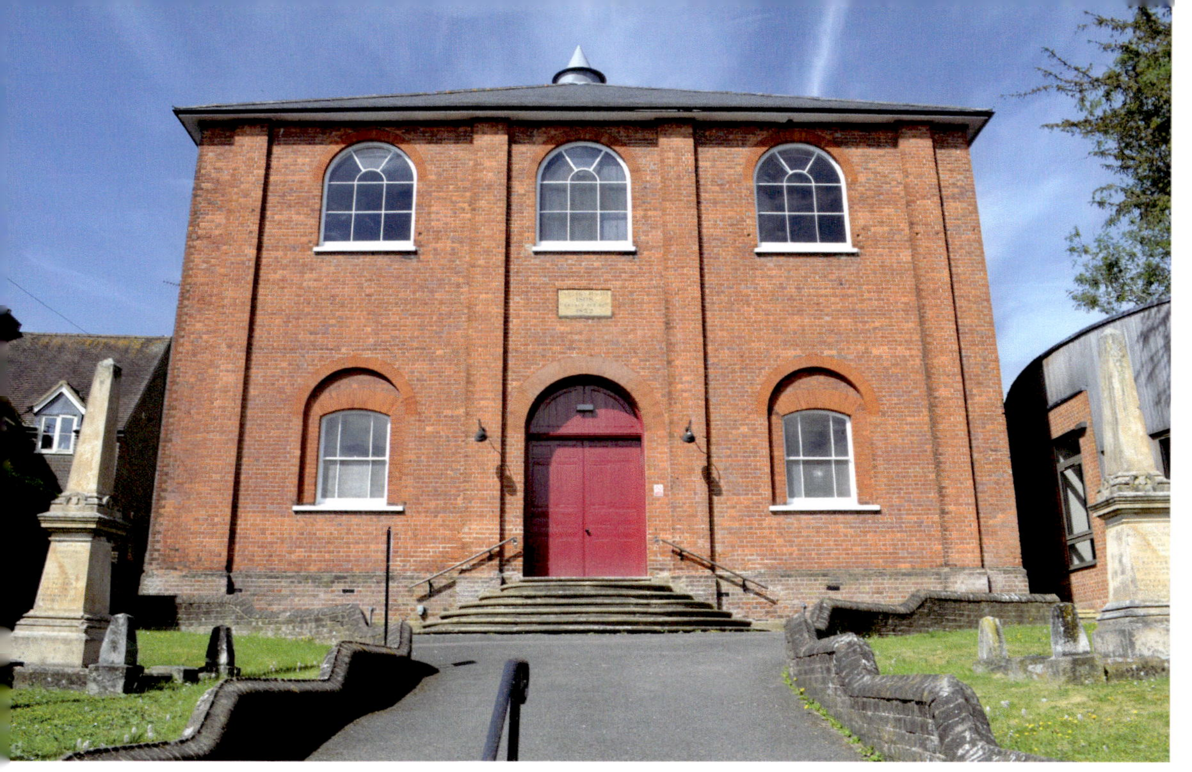

The Baptist chapel on Akeman Street.

communal facilities and a school hall by William Huckvale. Around the turn of the century the present organ was installed, and the brick boundary wall and steps were built. In *c.* 1908 all the timber windows were replaced – with a design that was probably similar to the original fenestration – and the brick porch was built onto the north-east entrance of the school hall. In the same year the chapel gallery was rebuilt, wainscoting was added to the ground floor, and the rostrum was replaced. In 2016 a single-storey extension was built on the north side.

The building is now Grade II listed, primarily for its architectural interest, but partly due to Tring being notable for the strength of its Baptist tradition.

14. High Street Banks

The former NatWest bank on the High Street was built in the 1830s by the Butcher family as the Tring Bank and the adjacent former HSBC was designed for the Midland Bank by architects Gotch and Saunders. On the corner of Bank Alley is a lump of masonry which was said to be a precaution against robbers.

Thomas Butcher's parents came to the town in the early nineteenth century, and set up business in a small way as grocers and tallow chandlers. Their son branched into dealing in seed and corn, prospering sufficiently to found 'a bank of issue' (a bank that has the official right to produce currency) in 1836, going on to build fine new premises in what later became the National Westminster Bank in the Lower High Street. At this date, many small market towns could support a

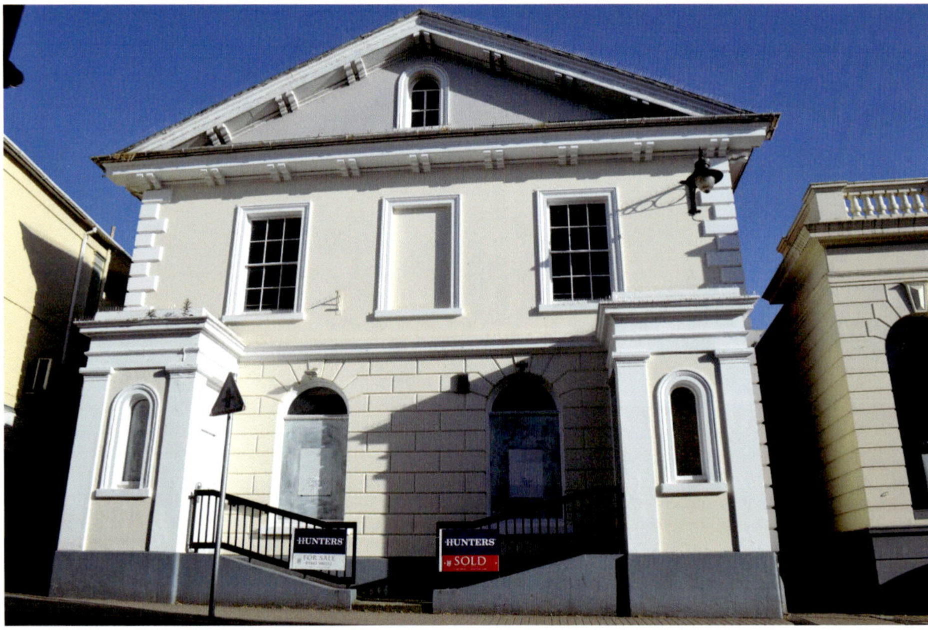

Above: The former NatWest bank, a sign of the times that it now awaits a future use.

Below: The former HSBC bank along with the closed NatWest bank.

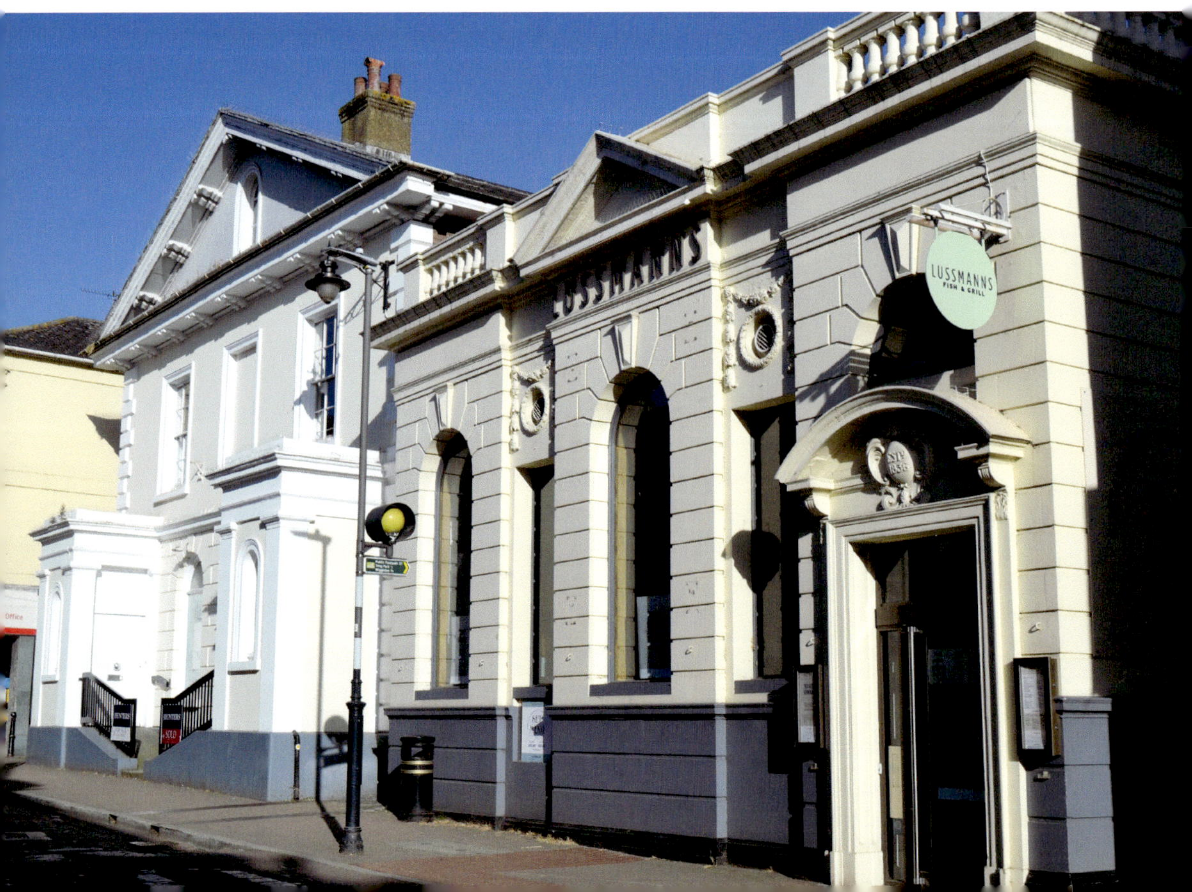

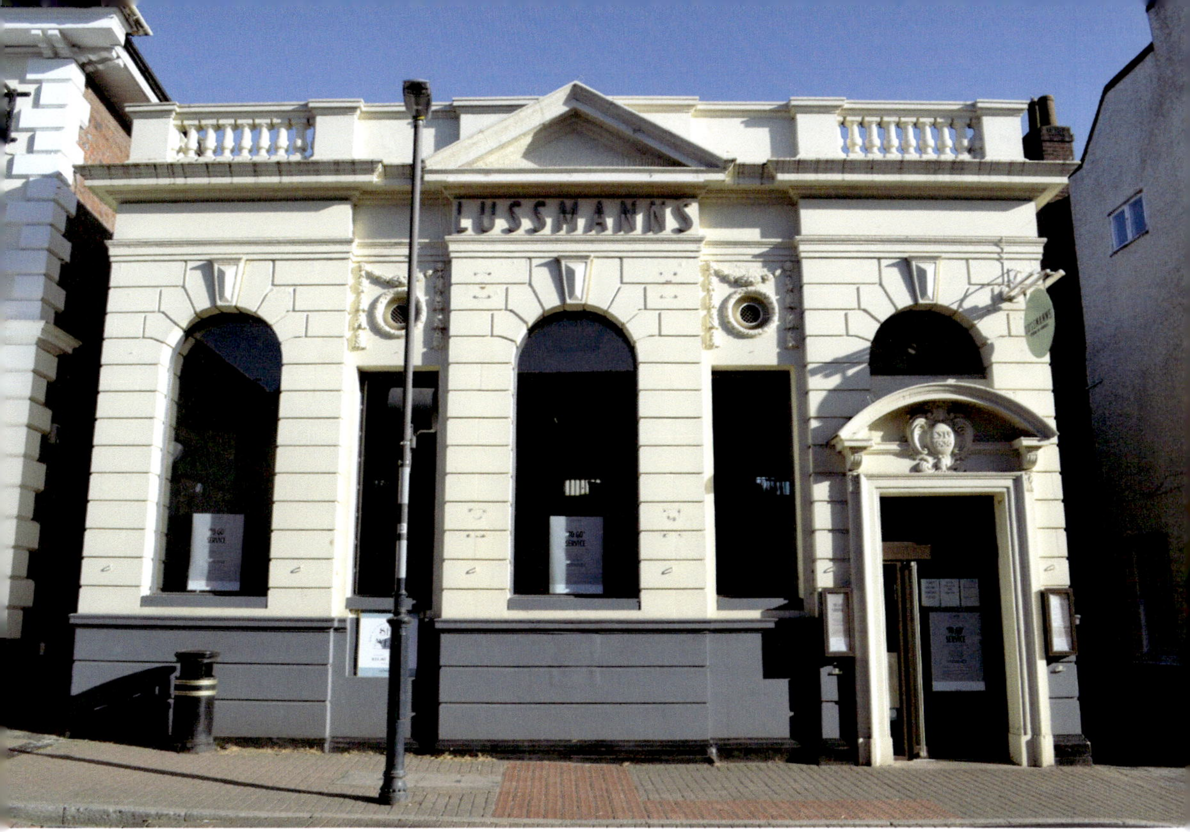

The former HSBC bank, designed by architect J. A. Gotch, who designed many buildings for the former Midland Bank.

private bank, and the profits enabled Thomas and his sons to invest, as did many successful businessmen, in land and property.

Thus there arose in this 'highly industrious and thriving little town' a need for banking facilities in an age before the appearance of modern high-street banks. Nonconformists were prominent among those who set up in business as bankers, for being barred from a wide range of careers by the discriminatory legislation of the era they concentrated their energies on trade and commerce. The Butcher family were businessmen, dealing in groceries, tea, tallow, seeds and corn. They were also Nonconformists, Strict Baptists, and so extending the family's business activities into banking was not so unusual in that era. The bank was also represented at Aylesbury and Chesham on market days. The bank's business was mainly agricultural and it is said that local farmers and merchants used to accompany the partners, acting as their escorts, when conducting banking business in nearby towns.

John Alfred Gotch (1852–1942) was born in Kettering and was a notable architect. His impact on the town of Kettering was considerable. Following the end of the war, Gotch's practice designed and built over 140 branches of Midland Bank and, in association with Edwin Lutyens, Gotch designed the interior of the bank's former headquarters in Poultry, London, which is today considered an art deco icon.

15. The Silk Mill, Brook Street

As you pass through Tring, along Brook Street, there is a small industrial complex called the Silk Mill, which has played a major part in the history of Tring and forms a fine complex of buildings today. In 1824, the largest and most successful operation of all was set up and financed by an astute businessman and entrepreneur, William Kay.

It was money generated by the silk trade that supplied another direct connection to Tring. The Williams family, who acquired the Pendley Manor estate, had inherited a fortune from profits amassed in the manufacture of a specialised type of silk. The founder of the family, Joseph Grout, probably started to trade in Spitalfields, and with his brother invented or learned a way of making black embossed silk crêpe. The obsession of the nineteenth century with mourning attire, popularised in large measure by Queen Victoria after the death of the Prince Consort, led to huge sales of this particular textile.

The factory Joseph established in Norwich prospered, and received the royal warrant in 1895. During the Second World War, it was one of only two firms to make parachute silk for the government, but ceased trading in the 1990s, 189 years after the Grout brothers first established the business. William Kay typified the go-ahead ambitious man who seized his chance to make money on the back of the Industrial Revolution. Using wealth made in the textile trade in Manchester,

Silk Mill Business Park, once a silk mill. It was originally two storeys taller.

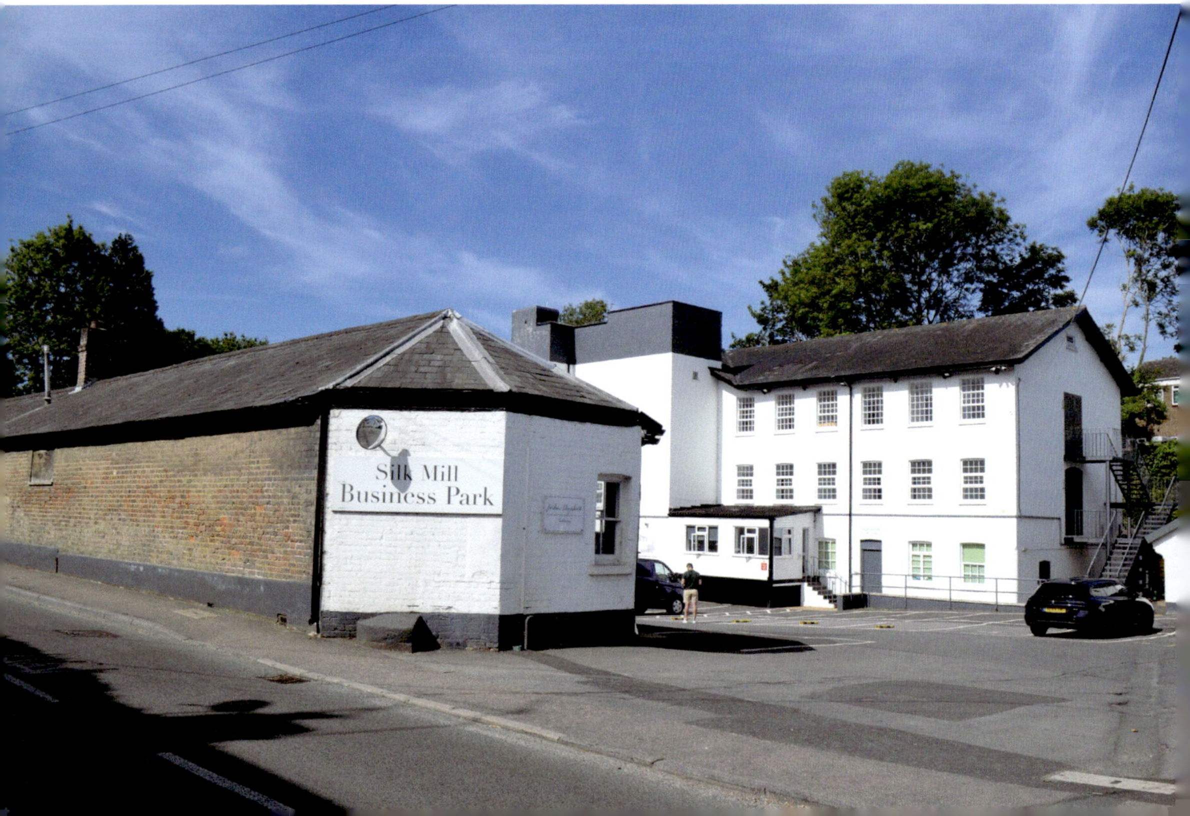

he moved south to London where he increased his fortune through his dealings in the Stock Exchange.

It is likely that William Kay selected Tring in which to invest because of its proximity to the capital, as well as the potential of the Brook End site, with its adjacent source of water power. After his arrival in the town he wasted no time in investigating the advantages of his new purchase, and within a year, the building of the Silk Mill was under way, in addition to a row of cottages on the west side of Brook Street. The setting up of the operation he entrusted to Joseph, and when the local populace nicknamed the looming five-storey mill 'Little Manchester', the Kay brothers most likely felt they had achieved their objective.

Although the mill has been much altered and enlarged over the years, it is apparent that William Kay was an ambitious builder as reference to old maps show that his plans produced an extensive L-shaped structure. Built of brick, five storeys high, and with a small warehouse on each floor, at each level the floors were supported by runs of evenly spaced cast-iron pillars, and through the centre of the building ran a central staircase. The ground floor housed a dining room for the workers, and offices, one of which was occupied by Joseph Parker, a key member of staff whose position today would be described as chief accountant.

The engine house was approached by an oilcloth-covered stairway, with the chimneystack adjoining the main building. Outside were the carpenters' and mechanics' workshops, the silk washing room, and two warehouses. As was

Once a workplace for over 500 people, including 320 children.

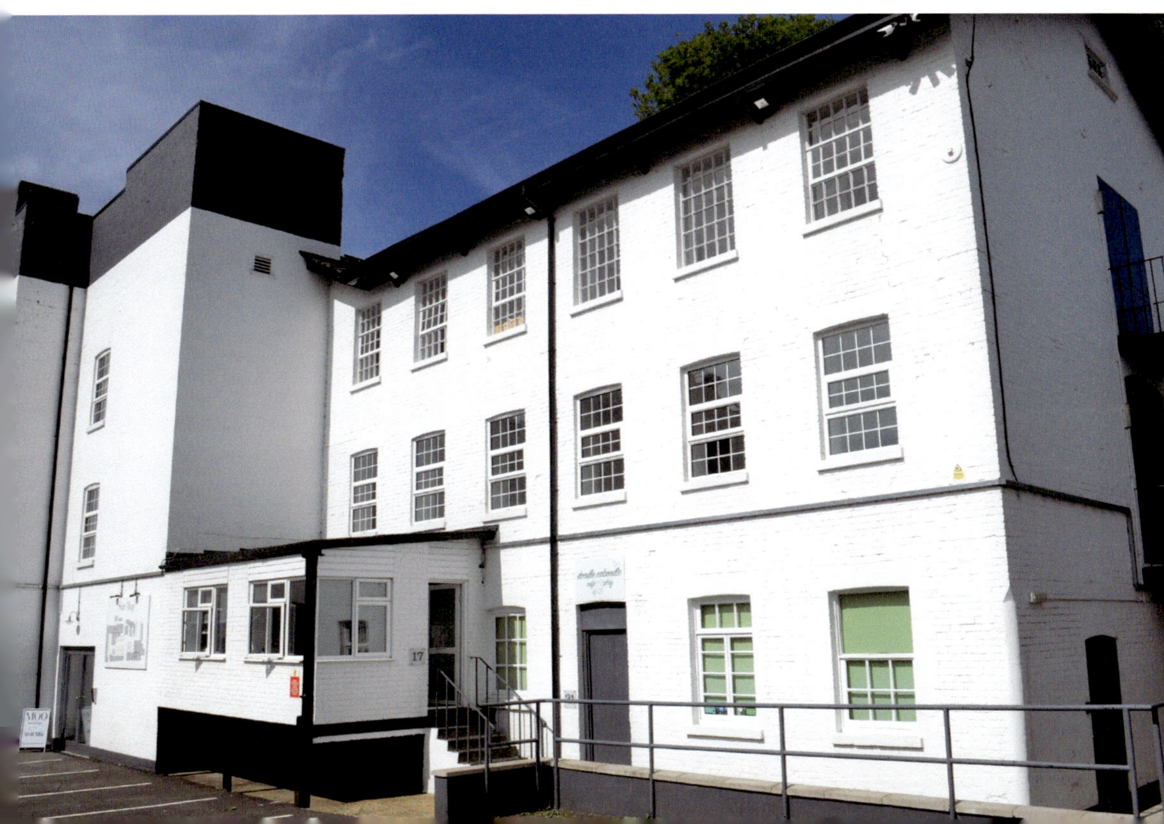

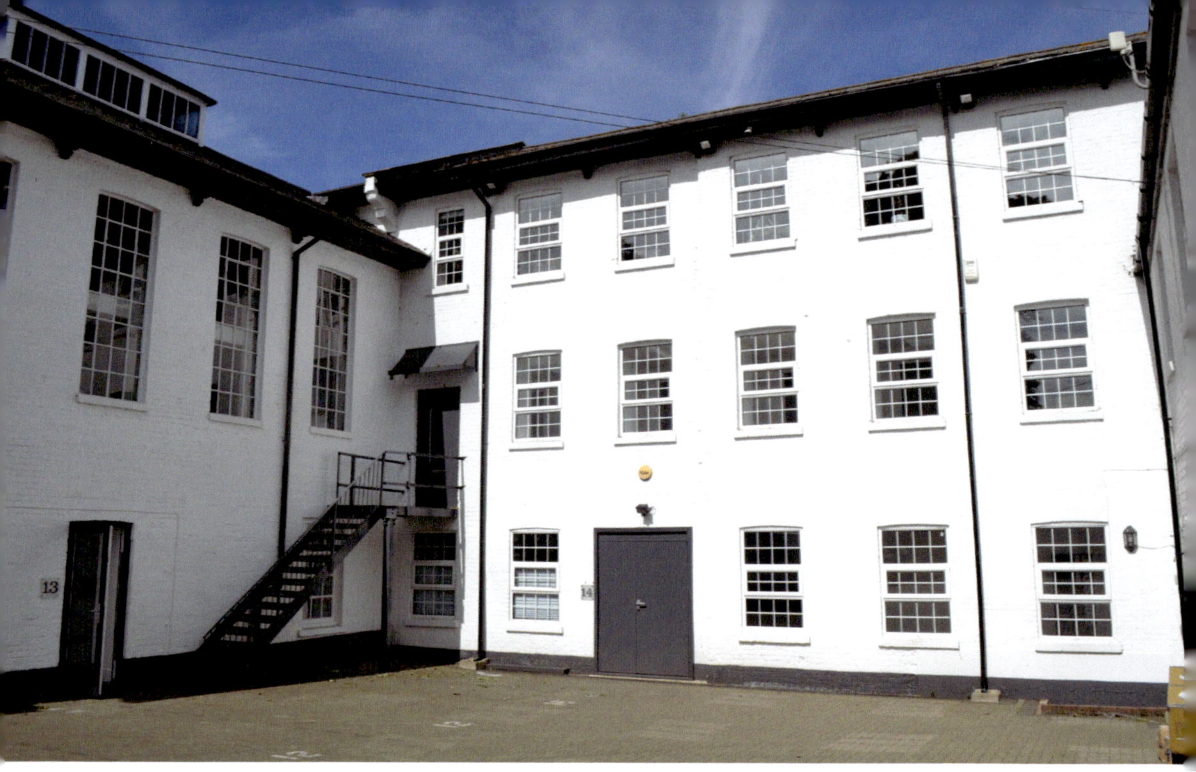

Converted into workshops and businesses today.

customary, accommodation was provided for the senior staff: a large house and garden for the manager, a good-sized cottage, and a lodge house. Other amenities included stabling for three horses, a double coach-house and a smith's shop and forge.

Descriptions of the numbers employed in the mill vary greatly and fluctuated according to the demand for the supply of silk and to agricultural seasonal work. In 1840 a reliable account states that the mill had capacity for 500 pairs of hands, consisting of 40 men, 140 women and 320 children. The superintendents received one pound a week; the men between 12 and 15 shillings; the average women's wages were 5*s* 6*d*; and the children's between 1*s* 0*d* and 2*s* 3*d*.

All in all, it was probably a good thing that William Kay established the silk industry in Tring, as it gave employment to many in the town, either directly or indirectly.

16. Former Royal Hotel

The London to Birmingham Railway was built by Robert Stephenson, and was the first line built out of London. Where it crossed the Chiltern Hills a very significant cutting was excavated at Tring, initially for two lines, but later widened to carry four. It became part of the London & North Western Railway in 1846. Tring station opened in 1837 and its rural situation required services to be available and the brother of William Brown, the auctioneer, opened the impressive adjacent hotel, originally named The Harcourt Arms, the following year. This provided

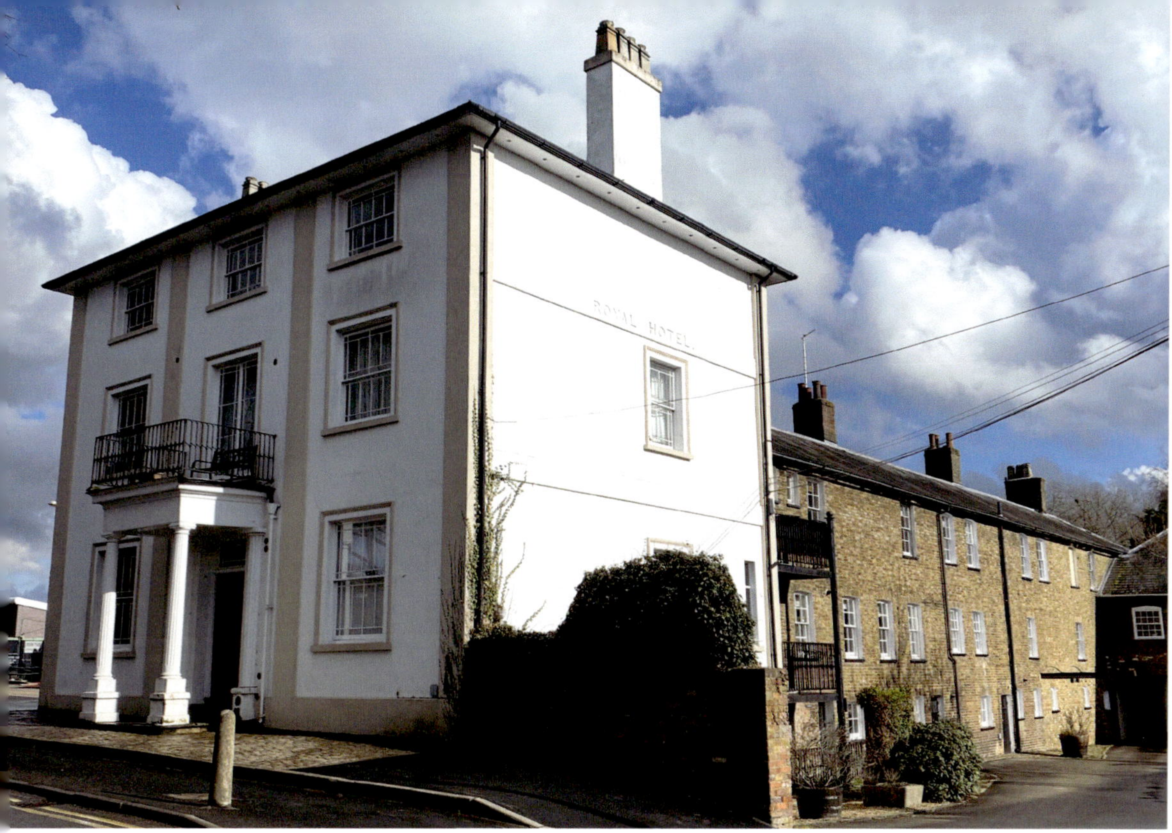

The former Royal Hotel, once a posting house.

food, drink, accommodation and horse transport for arriving passengers. To speed the journey between the town and the station a new road was constructed, Station Road, bypassing Pendley.

John Brown, brewer of Tring, under arrangement with the London & Birmingham Railway Company, was responsible for this former hotel. The south wing was rebuilt in brick in the 1860s for Lord Lonsdale and further modified in 1937. Its name was changed between 1845 and 1851 to The Royal Hotel. Demand for this sort of facility probably declined with the advent of motor transport and it is no longer a hotel today but residential. From the 1881 Census, the hotel keeper was Samuel Brown, aged thirty-five, born in Okeford Fitzpaine, Dorset. His wife was Jane M. Brown, aged thirty-two, born in Stoke Prior, Worcestershire. Other residents included their son Ernest S. Brown, aged eleven, one cook, one chambermaid, one barmaid, one ostler, one waiter, and one post boy.

17. Goldfield Mill

Goldfield Mill is a four-storey former tower mill which had a pepperpot cap winded by a fantail. There were four double patent sails with an upright shaft and a cast-iron great spur wheel. It was first mentioned in Pigot's Directory of 1839 when James Grover was the miller. Grover was a partner with the Mead family of the Mead Flour Mill in New Mill. After a disagreement with the family, he built the mill to continue in business on his own. The mill remained in the Grover family until 1880.

The Grovers' tenancy was not without its controversy. In 1862 James Grover died and the partnership between father and sons was dissolved. Jabez and William parted company, with William remaining as miller. The reason for this parting, which has long persisted in local folklore, was that the brothers quarreled violently, which led to William murdering Jabez with a coal shovel; thereafter his ghost was said to haunt the staircase of the Mill House. But although William might well have crowned Jabez with a shovel, there are no reports of this allegedly grisly event in newspapers of the time and it is likely that Jabez died peacefully in his bed, for the grave of a Jabez Grover, dated 1889, can be seen in New Mill Chapel burial ground.

By 1898, a 6-horsepower (4.5-kW) steam engine had been installed as auxiliary power. During Thomas Liddington's tenure of the mill, miller Henry Liddington was fined £10 for taking an excessive toll of flour. The Liddingtons also had their problems during their operations at the mill. Although not recorded, it does appear that Thomas Liddington bought the property. This proved to be a poor investment, for by this time milling was becoming a highly mechanised trade and as the years passed Goldfield windmill could not compete favourably in the flour trade with Thomas Mead's increasingly modern steam mill at Gamnel Wharf. In 1888 Thomas Liddington was forced to file for bankruptcy, the application being heard in Aylesbury County Court where it was recorded that his liabilities amounted to 1,176. 3*s* 3*d*, with a deficiency of £269 11*s* 7*d*. Described as a miller and farmer, Thomas claimed that the causes of his failure were a decline in trade, bad debts and other losses incurred due to his horse and cattle dying. But this was not the only disaster to befall the Liddington family, for Henry's dealings with customers were not always scrupulously honest.

Who held the mill during the next few years is unknown, but after 1888 it was worked by White & Putnam, a partnership that operated several local mills. At some stage, James Wright, the miller at Hastoe steam mill, about a mile and a half from Tring, took over at Goldfield. He is shown as being a miller at both sites until about 1902, by which time he had moved to Goldfield.

The viability of the mill at this time appears to have depended largely upon a contract with the Rothschild Tring Park estate for crushing oats for animal feed on its many farms. The contract ending in 1908, James left Goldfield to take over the tenancy of Brook End water and steam mill situated some 3 miles away on the border of Ivinghoe and Pitstone, taking its water supply from the Whistle Brook. He is recorded here in 1911 as a miller, baker and confectioner, but was forced to give up in 1913, being unable to compete with the large milling firms.

Goldfield mill was then put up for auction by William Brown & Co., the *Bucks Herald* reporting that 'Considerable interest was manifested in Tring and the surrounding district regarding the sale of Goldfield Windmill, one of the most well-known landmarks in the neighbourhood. The property comprised the windmill; two dwelling houses; numerous outbuildings; and a valuable meadow of about two acres, with a long frontage to Miswell Lane. The property stands at a high and healthy elevation and commands the most perfect scenery of the Vale of Aylesbury and the Chiltern Hills, and the downs and woodlands of the Ashridge estate. Messrs. W. Brown & Co. submitted the whole property by auction on October 30th but the bidding did not reach the reserve figure and is now to be dealt with privately.'

In 1911 Brown & Co. again advertised the complex, but the outcome is unknown. It is likely that milling had ceased following James Wright's departure, for by this time small milling concerns saw their business dwindling in the face of competition from much larger and more efficient roller mills. However, the living accommodation at Goldfield continued to be used and Miriam Wright, who in the period 1916–21 lived with her parents in one of the cottages, remembered that during the First World War, soldiers used the top windows of the mill for signal practice.

In 1919, the entire complex was eventually sold for, it is believed, £1,000 to a Mrs Cunningham from Rhodesia. This lady then constructed a dwelling for herself and her family in the granary and attached cottage, later turning the barn into a bungalow for her daughter. When Mrs Cunningham died in 1955, the house passed to Peter Bell, a journalist for the *British Farmer and Stockbreeder* magazine, but the windmill continued in its state of dereliction.

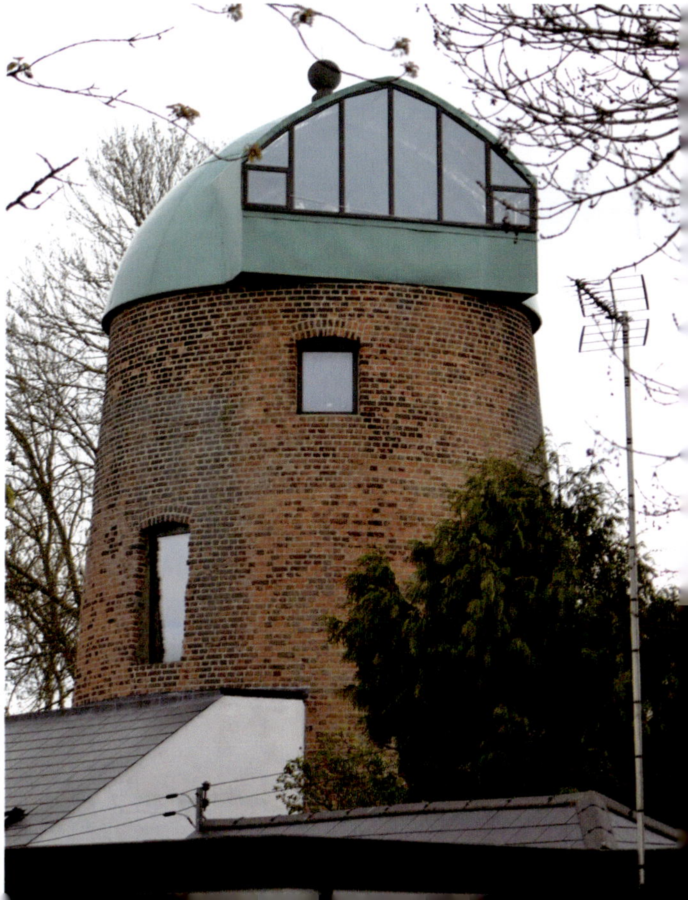

The mill, now converted into a rather fine residence.

In 1946 the tenancy of the adjacent Mill House cottage was acquired by a well-known local lady Phyllis Thomas, librarian at the Akeman Street Zoological Museum, who lived there for many years until forced to leave by her increasing frailty (she died in 1990 aged 102).

The Mill House and its adjoining granary now form a single dwelling, sympathetically restored and modernised by its present owners. Goldfield windmill now claims the distinction of a Grade II listing, as well as being the only remaining tower mill in Dacorum.

18. The Anchor Public House, Western Road

The Anchor is one of the more popular public houses in Tring and is one of the oldest to survive in the town today. The population censuses capture the many publicans who have held court here. In 1841, the proprietors were George and Lydia Barber along with their three children, Sarah, Alfred and Emma. At the time, George was described as a 'cotton weaver and beer shop keeper'. The 1871 census still records them as living here, with George described as a weaver, and his wife as a straw plaiter, and now have their three-year-old granddaughter, Emma, living with them.

By 1881, the pub was known as the Anchor Arms public house and James Webb was now publican, along with his wife, Elizabeth. Ten years later, sixty-year-old Alfred Barber was the beerhouse keeper, the son of George and Lydia, and is living with his wife Jane. In the 1901 census, it is known as The Anchor and the publican was fifty-four-year-old William Wells and a housekeeper called Mary. It appears that William eventually married Mary, fourteen years younger than him. The *Bucks Herald* of 6 November 1909 reported: 'The death of Mr. W. Wells. The death on Wednesday 27th ult. Of Mr William Wells, for some years the licensee of The Anchor Public House. Mr Wells has been in failing health for the past two years and during the last few months has been afflicted with dropsy. On September 21st a report said "Marriage of Mrs Wells. At the Parish Church on Wednesday afternoon Mrs Wells, the well-known hostess of The Anchor, married Mr William Bell of Deptford. The ceremony was conducted by the Rev. D.F. Slemeck. Two of the bride's nieces were bridesmaids"'. However, the marriage was, sadly, not a long one. The *Bucks Herald* of 8 April 1916 reported, 'On Monday evening Mr William Bell of the Anchor, Western Road, was engaged in serving customers when he reeled, fell face forward and suddenly expired.' Mary continued as hostess for another two years when the licence was transferred to William John Andrews. William died in April 1939, having been employed by Meads Flour Mills.

Today, The Anchor is the only pub that has survived on Western Road. This was despite the closure of the Tring bus garage, which was on the opposite side of the road. It closed in 1977 with considerable local bitterness at the loss of

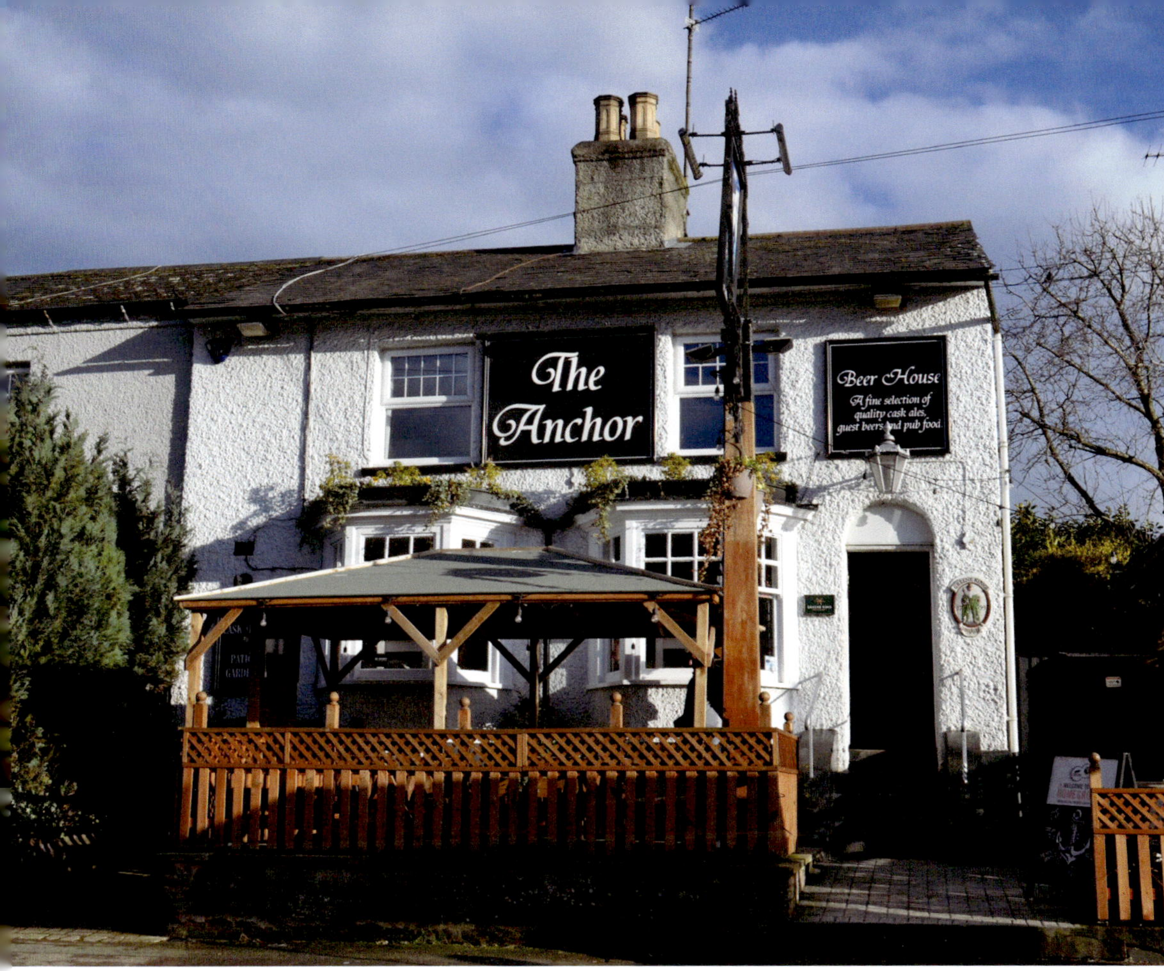

The Anchor public house, with its obtrusive wooden shelter to the front.

forty drivers based in Tring, four conductors and seven engineers. Such a loss of a local clientele could have meant the end of The Anchor, but it remains to this day.

19. The Former Britannia Public House, Now Norfolk House, Western Road

The former Britannia public house is now known as Norfolk House, and is a notable building as you come into Tring from the direction of Aylesbury. It was, however, a public house built primarily to cater for the navies working on the London to Birmingham railway, by John Brown of Tring Brewery. The census again provides details of ownership over the many years it was a public house. In 1841, in the area then known as Bottle Cross, it was run by thirty-five-year-old Henry Tompkins, with his wife, Mary, and his ten-year-old son, Thomas. By 1861 the Britannia had John Ray from Adstock as the named innkeeper with his wife, Elizabeth, and four sons.

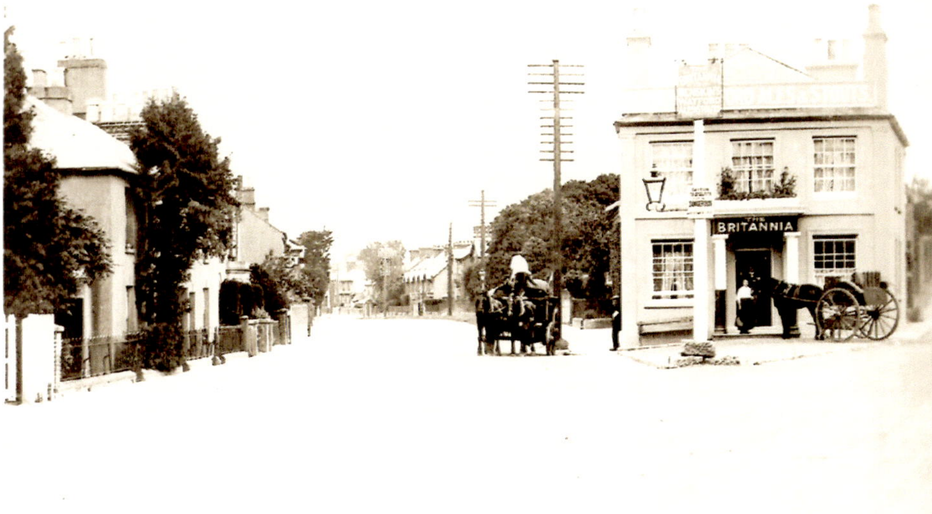

Above: The Britannia on Western Road, built by John Brown's brewery.

Below: The former pub is now a private residence called Norfolk House.

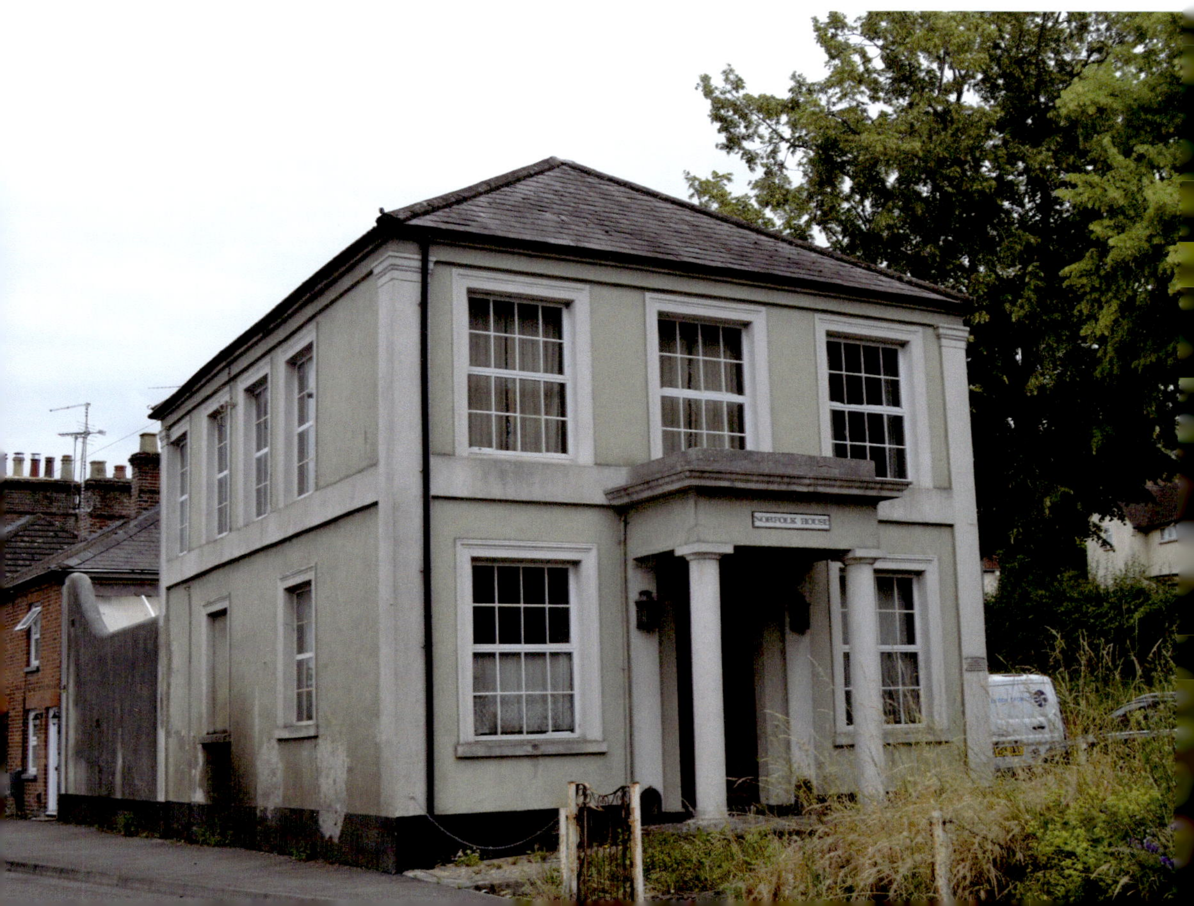

As with many public houses of the time, drunkenness and disorderliness were common. The Britannia was no different and it was reported on 25 August 1894 when Herbert Budd of Tring was charged with being drunk there on 11 August and Joseph Watson, the landlord, was charged with serving liquor to a drunken man. Thankfully for Watson, the case was dismissed but he did receive a warning.

In 1900, it was Queen Victoria's eighty-first birthday, which was celebrated by a cycle parade from the Britannia at 9 o'clock and reported in the paper of 2 June. Nearly one hundred cyclists took part.

The triangular piece of land in front of the public house has been the centre of controversy over many years. John Brown was adamant that it belonged to him and marked it out with kerbs to indicate that it was not public land. Even discussions with the council and the brewers did not resolve this and it remained as an open space. In 1913, there were further issues when a 5-ton lorry loaded with 5 tons of paper for Hazel, Watson and Viney, from Aylesbury, got stuck on the open space, sinking into the earth, taking many hours to get it released and unstuck. The open space remains to this day.

In early years, the Britannia was a turning point for local buses, later extended to the nearby cemetery with the local paper reporting: 'Buses will now start at the Rose and Crown and not the Britannia, causing inconvenience to those living in the West End'. The Britannia remained a popular public house well into the twentieth century but was sadly closed in about 1978 as there were no inside toilets and those outside were deemed unsuitable by the local authority. It was bought in 1980 and converted into a residential property by Christmas 1982 and renamed Norfolk House.

2c. The Castle, Park Road

The Castle is one of the most popular public houses in Tring, situated on Park Road with fine views across the Downs. It was first mentioned in the 1861 census when it was described as 'a beer shop in West Park Street'. John Woodhouse, an engineer and beer retailer, was living here with his wife Isabella and five children. In the 1867 trade directory, George Rance was there, but by 1871, the pub was being run by twenty-five-year-old William Lloyd from London, with his wife, Harriet, and son, William. They were there for many years and still recorded as living here in 1891 as he was injured in a serious accident. In 1887, plans were put forward for a stable to be built here. The *Bucks Herald* of 15 August 1891 recorded poor William's unfortunate accident. 'Mr William Lloyd of The Castle Inn has this week met with a serious accident. He was taking a load up the Crong Hill and shutting out his horse to go back to the assistance of one of his men whose horse had a heavier load when the shafts suddenly flew up into the air. Mr Lloyd was lifted off his feet and thrown down, sustaining a fracture of the

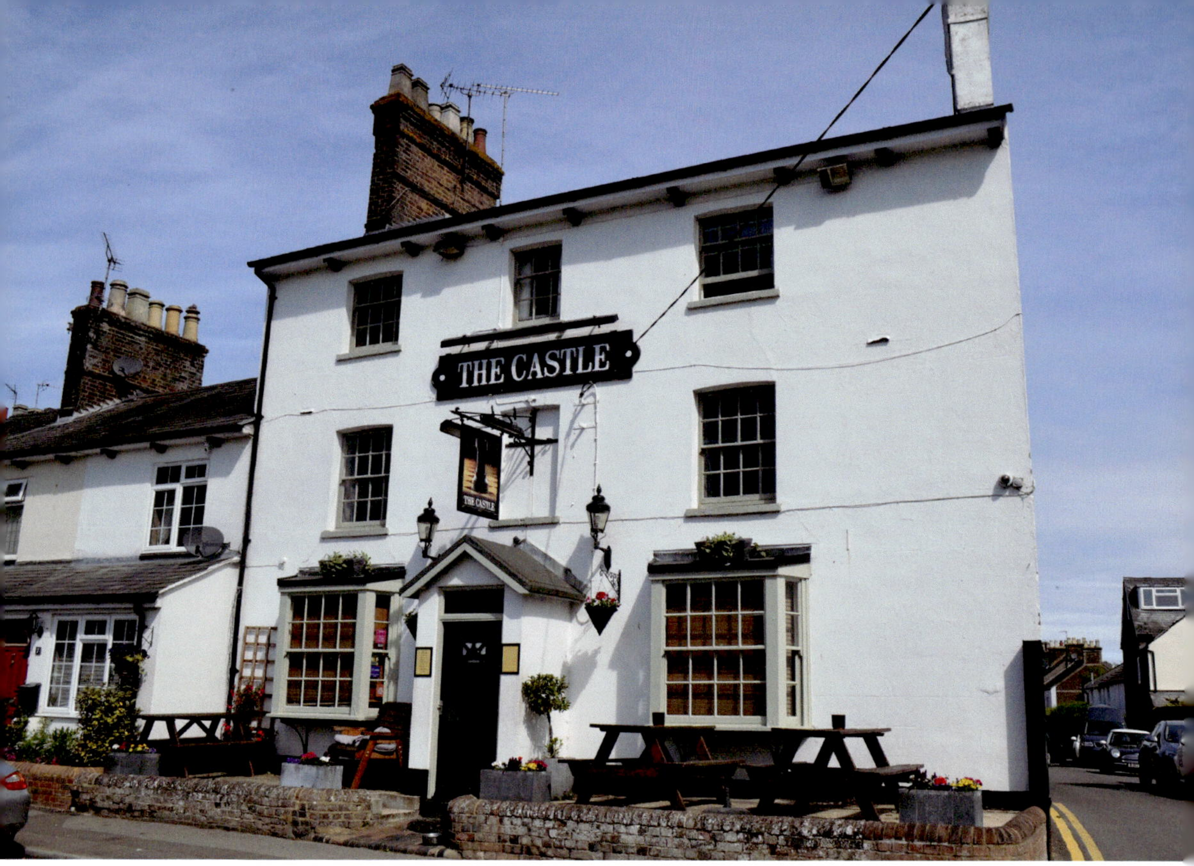

The Castle, described once as a 'beer shop'.

leg.' The census of 1891 described William as a 'timber carrier', clearly a risky occupation. William died in August 1895, at the young age of fifty years old.

The Castle was taken over by Robert Ives, fifty-eight years old, in 1901, who was described as a carpenter and publican. The grandly named Ephraim Hearn was the publican in the 1930s.

21. Vestry Hall, Church Yard

This was where the town's first administrative body held meetings. It remains the home of Tring Charities, which distributes the proceeds of ancient bequests to the poor and needy of today. It is interesting to look back at the street parties held in Tring for Queen Elizabeth II's coronation in 1953. The party held in Church Lane was given high praise by the *Bucks Herald*.

'Church Lane is probably Tring's smallest thoroughfare, but it deserved a big hand for its decorations and illuminations. The folk who live in the Lane were justifiably proud of their display, and they certainly set the rest of the town a patriotic example. When they held their celebration on Saturday the Vicar the Rev. T.K. Lowdell came as guest – about forty children, old folk and helpers had tea in the Vestry Hall'. Much of Church Lane was demolished to make way for Dolphin

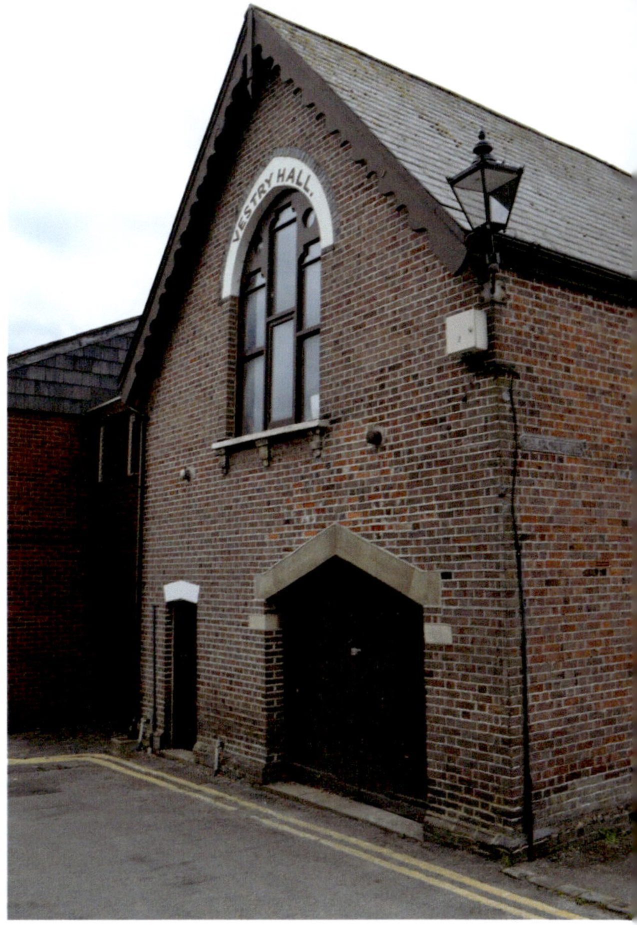

The old Vestry building, which has served the town over many decades including housing a horse-drawn fire engine, and as a police station.

Square. Vestry Hall thankfully remained and is a reminder of the town's civic functions. Built in about 1866, it once housed Tring's horse-drawn fire engine and was also used as a police station until the new one was ready on the High Street.

22. Pendley Manor

Located on the edge of Tring is the rather fine Pendley Manor. Pendley (or Penley, Pendele, or Pentlai) dates back to the fourth century AD, held in the 'honour of Berkhampstead'. The manor of Pendley predates the Norman Conquest of 1066, after which it was confiscated by William the Conqueror and passed to his brother-in-law, Robert, Count of Mortain, who became one of the greatest landholders in the newly conquered Kingdom of England. A later owner was John de Angle, an early Member of Parliament.

By the fifteenth century, Pendley was a small town. In 1440 the county sheriff of Essex and Hertfordshire, Sir Robert Whittingham (or Whytingham), and his wife Agnes received a grant of free warren from King Henry VI at Pendley manor; Sir Robert enclosed 200 acres and tore down the buildings on the land, returning the estate to pasture. It was here that he built a manor house at the western end of the now-demolished town as a double cloistered courtyard. Whittingham subsequently obtained a papal licence to build a chapel at the manor house and engage a priest to hold services there when the roads became impassable in winter.

On the accession of King Edward IV, Whittingham's fortunes changed; the king attained Whittingham for his loyalty to Henry and in 1461 he granted Pendley Manor to George Neville, Bishop of Exeter. Around 1472, Whittingham's daughter Margaret married John Verney, son of a Lord Mayor of London, Sir Ralph de Verney. Because of the king's favour for Verney, he lifted the attainder on Whittingham and Pendley Manor land passed to the Verney family.

The Verney family lived at the medieval manor for the next 150 years. The Anderson family then occupied it for four generations from 1606. In 1630, a friend of Sir Richard Anderson, Revd Lawrence Washington, visited Pendley Manor. During his stay there he became acquainted with Amphyllis Twigden and began a love affair with her. As a fellow of Brasenose College, Oxford, Washington was prohibited from marrying, and in 1631 Amphyllis bore him a son out of wedlock. Eventually Archbishop William Laud granted the couple a licence to marry, and Lawrence and Amphyllis were married in Tring in late 1632. Their son, John Washington, emigrated to Virginia in 1657. The Washington family became established in the new colony, and over a century later in 1789, John's great-grandson, George Washington, became the first President of the United States of America.

In 1677, Anderson's daughter Elizabeth married the politician Simon Harcourt. Sir Richard Anderson died in 1699, and he was buried in the Pendley Chapel in the

An early view of Pendley Manor from the air.

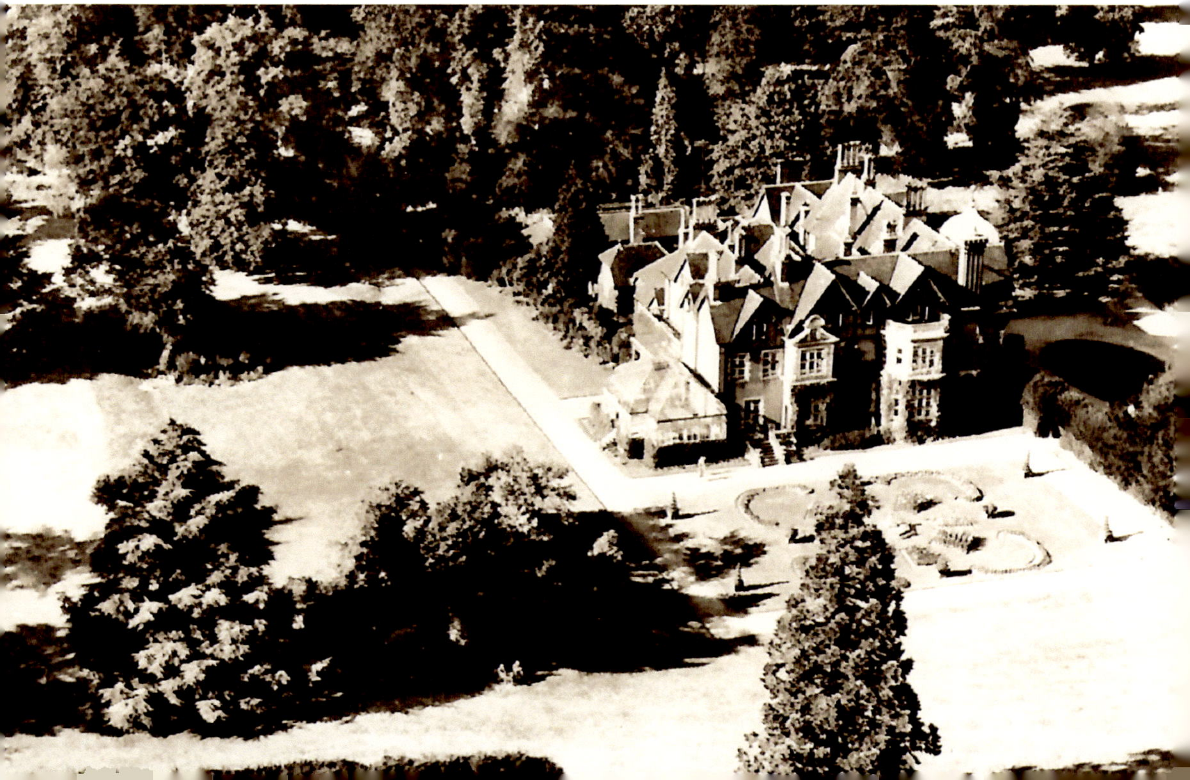

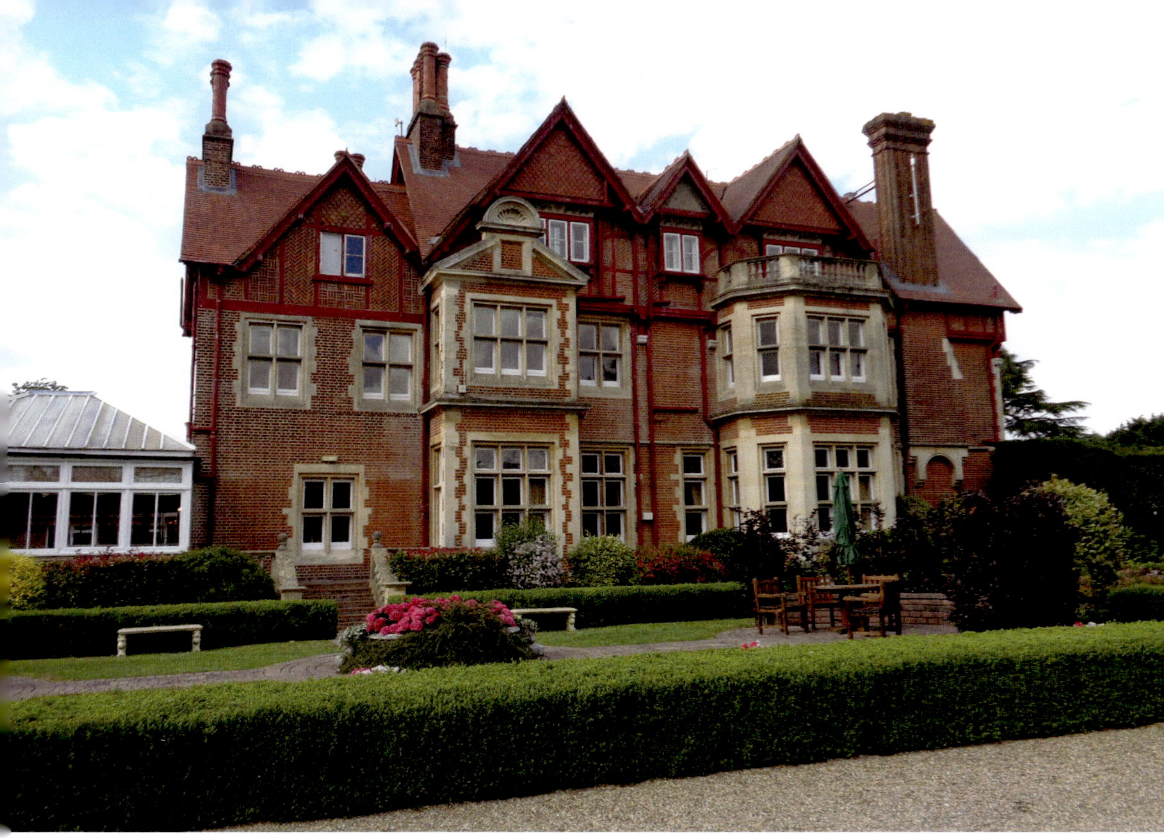

Pendley Manor, now a popular hotel. Its history and those who have lived here have formed a significant part of the town and its growth.

Church of St John the Baptist in the neighbouring village of Aldbury, alongside his wife Dame Elizabeth Anderson and their other children. As the young Elizabeth was the Anderson family's only surviving child, Pendley Manor passed through marriage to the Harcourt family.

In the 1830s, at the height of the Industrial Revolution, railway engineer Robert Stephenson began construction on the new London & Birmingham Railway. The project was delayed by opposition from local landowners (among them Lord Brownlow and Sir Astley Cooper); after a change in the planned route, parliamentary approval was granted, and the railway line was built along a route parallel to the Grand Junction Canal, some distance to the east of Tring – but too close to Pendley Manor to suit the occupant, Sir William Harcourt. He regarded the incursion of the iron horse into the locality as an intolerable nuisance and abandoned Pendley Manor. The ancient medieval manor buildings burnt down soon after in 1835.

Eventually, a local landowner, Joseph Grout Williams, commissioned architect Walter F. K. Lyon to build a new Tudor-style manor, the present building, in 1872. He and his descendants then occupied the Victorian manor from 1875 until 1983.

The last private owner was BBC show jumping commentator Dorian Williams, who developed it as a centre for adult education and the arts after the Second World War. He inaugurated the Pendley Open Air Shakespeare Festival in 1949

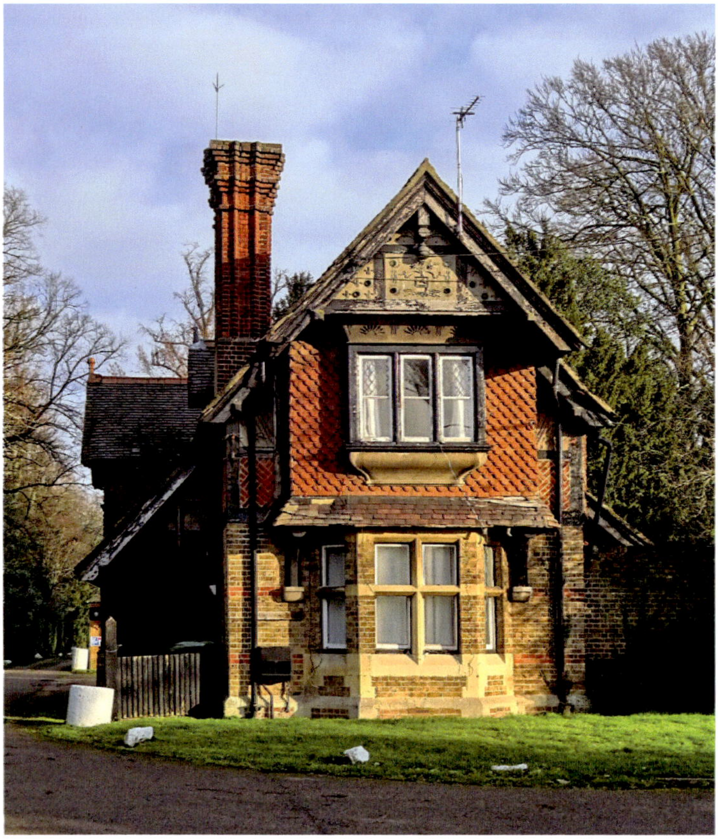

One of the lodges at the entrance to Pendley Manor.

in the hotel grounds, which continues to run to the present day. The grounds have two landscaped open-air stages. The indoor Court Theatre has occupied the former stables of the estate since 1978.

The house was sold to The Grass Roots Group in 1983 and then in 1989 to a hotel company which invested in the building and reopened it as a country house hotel in 1991. There have since been several extensions built to house additional rooms, a spa and gymnasium and a banqueting/conference suite.

23. Brown's Maltings

There are a number of courts off Akeman Street on both sides of the road. One of the more prominent ones is Rodwell Yard, containing Brown's Maltings. Rodwells was a long-established drinks business that had existed in Tring for over 150 years before moving to nearby Pitstone. Sadly it only lasted about ten years at its new address, failing in 2008. This yard was part of their premises before they moved. In 1876, Brown's Maltings occupied part of the site and has now lent its name to the refurbished buildings here. Maltings are buildings

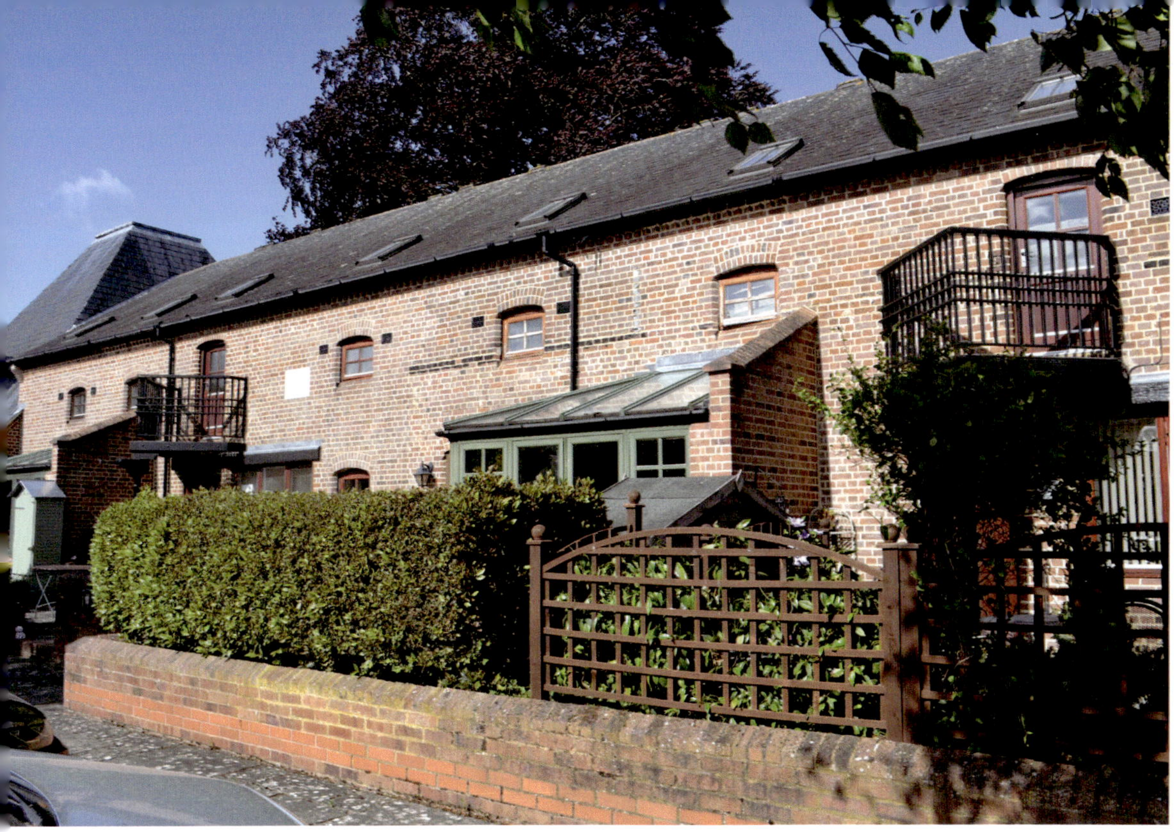

Above: The former Brown's Maltings.

Below: The old maltings, now residential.

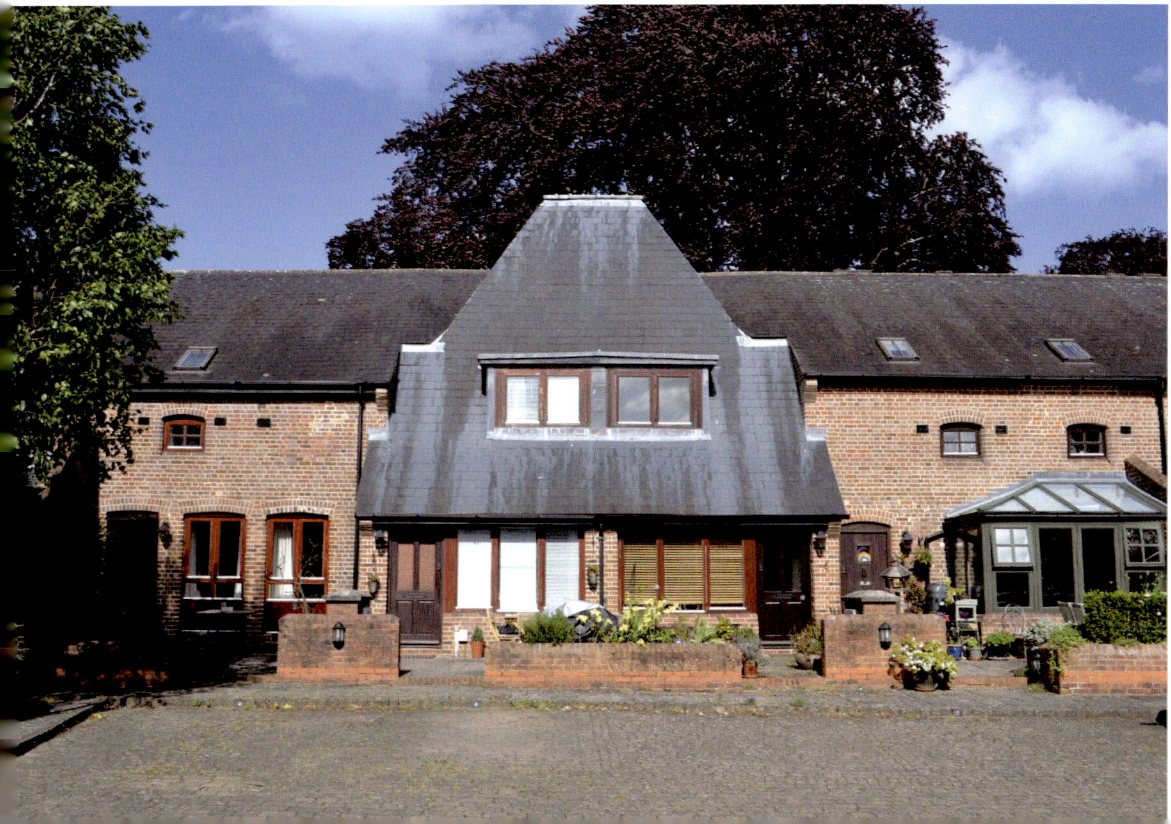

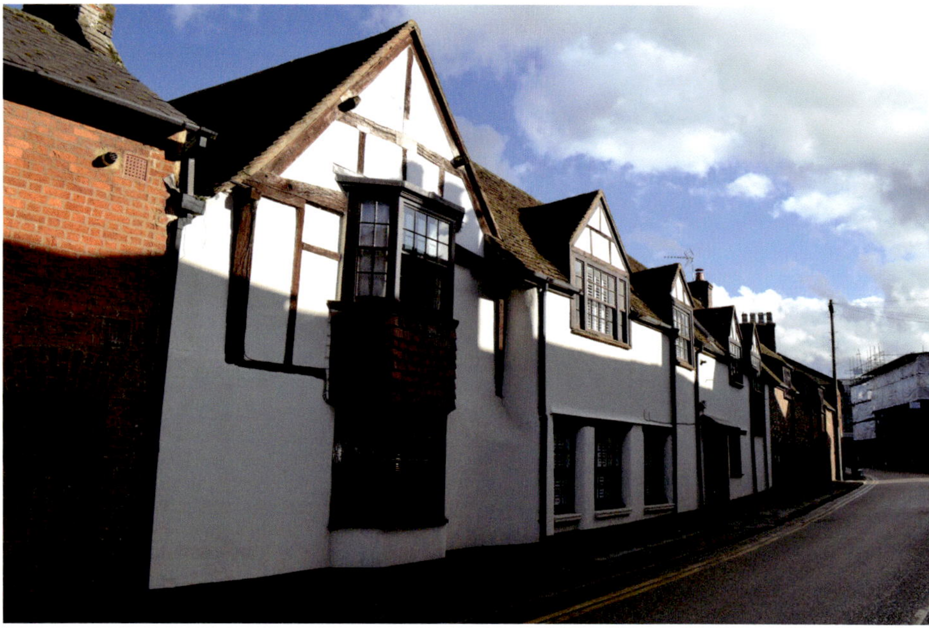

The former Grace's Maltings at No. 15 Akeman Street.

used to produce and store malt for use in the brewing industry. In the same street were also Grace's Maltings – the Grace's being another long-established Tring family, a branch of which still has a hardware shop on the High Street established well over 200 years ago.

24. Church of St Martha

The church of St Martha was originally built as a daughter church to St Peter and St Paul, in the centre of the town. Unfortunately it was never fully completed and therefore consecrated. It eventually became a chapel of ease (a building other than a parish church, built within the bounds of a parish for the attendance of those who cannot reach the parish church conveniently). It was built *c.* 1880, probably by Carpenter & Ingelow, who were working on the parish church at that time. It was built from the eastern end but never finished. It has a fine chancel of uncoursed flint with stone dressings and a steep-pitched red-tile roof. It is alleged to have stonework from the medieval parish church, which was redundant at restoration. Its full dedication may be to St Martha and St Mary.

The wooden structure was added about the turn of the twentieth century and a porch in the early 1960s. The Church of England membership was low in the 1970s, and use of the building was offered to the Methodist congregation and as the original Methodist chapel in Langdon Street was suffering from dry rot,

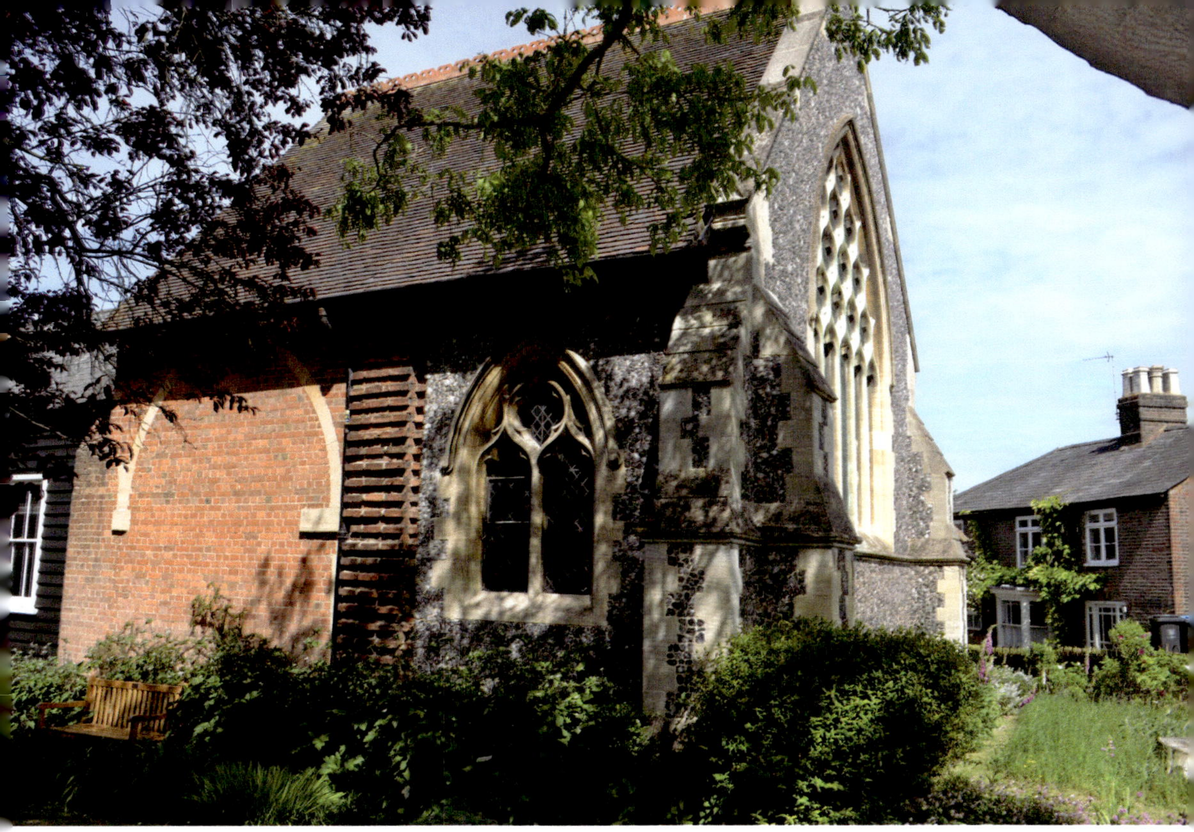

Above: The church of St Martha.

Below: The wooden extension, a later addition to the original church.

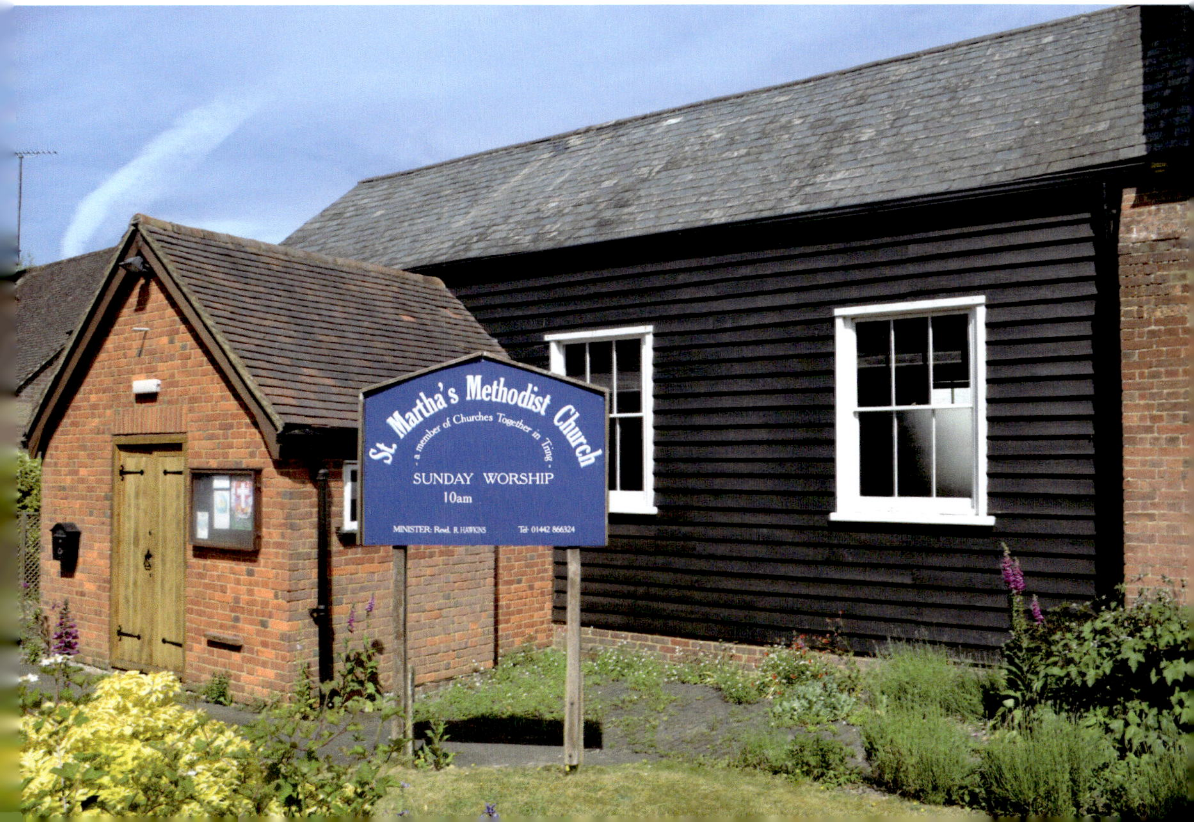

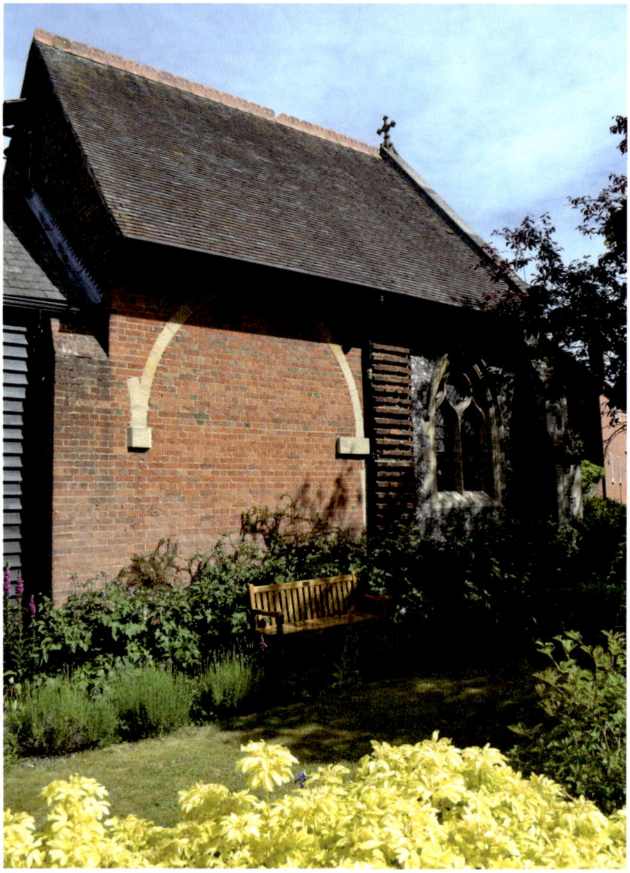

The church and its garden.

it was decided to abandon that building, and the money from the sale of the land was put towards the cost of a new joint Anglican/Methodist church hall, situated to the rear of the parish church. The church has been wholly Methodist-owned since 2002.

25. Grace Ironmongers, No. 68 High Street

Grace's seems to have been ever present in Tring for decades. They were established in 1750, and may actually have started out on Frogmore Street. Later, they had premises in Akeman Street. In the 1870s, Sebastian Grace also had premises near the Old Market House, in front of the church. In the 1880s, they were located at No. 34 High Street. They are seen here at No. 68 High Street (this part was originally called Western Road), built in 1890. Their influence on Tring was considerable, having been the manufacturers of many of the wrought-iron gates throughout the town, including substantial work for the Rothschilds in the construction of the museum.

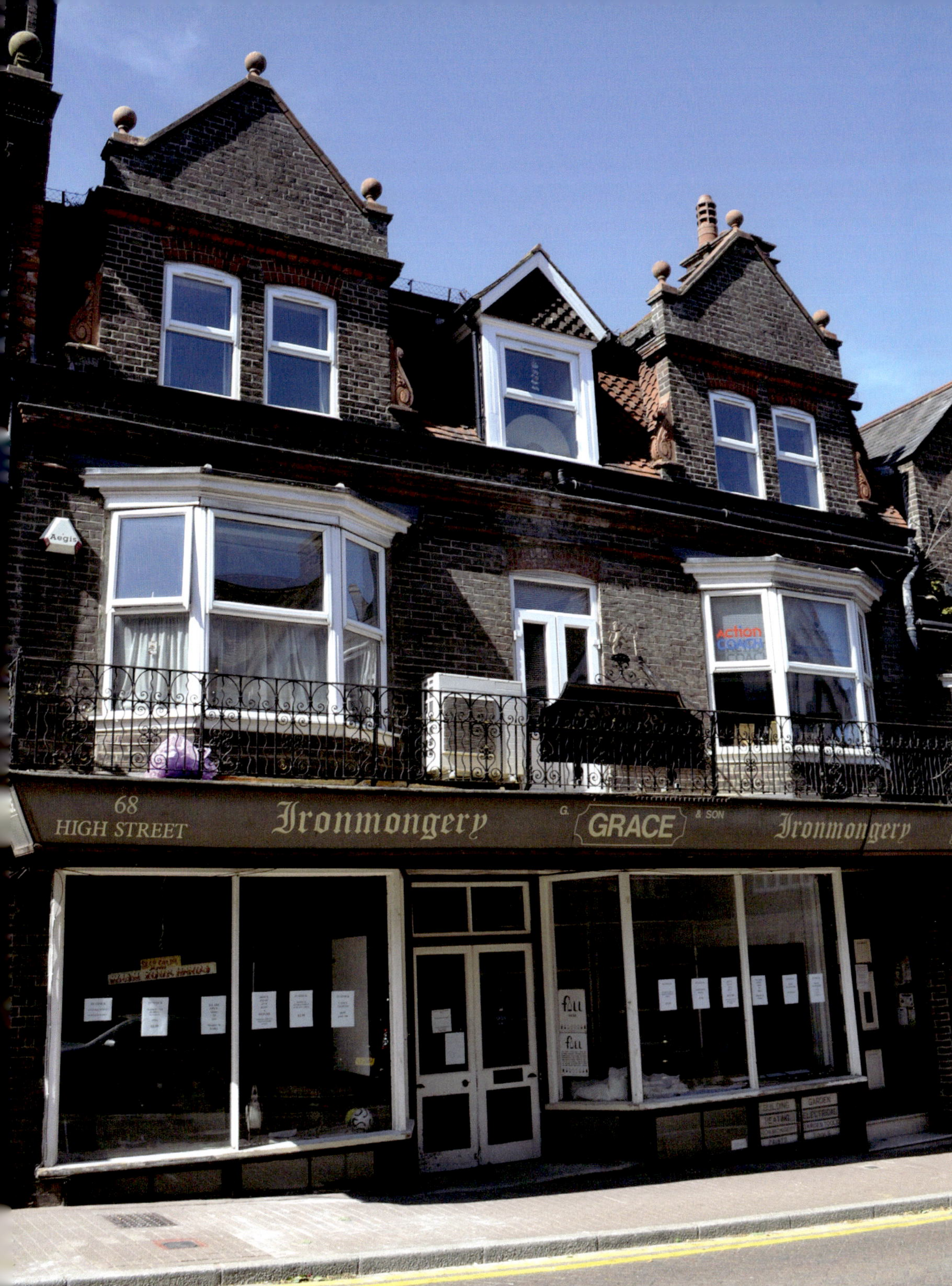

Grace Ironmongery, at No. 68 High Street. The firm was established in 1750.

26. Hastoe Village Hall

Towards the end of the nineteenth century, Emma, Lady Rothschild, created what has been described as 'a mini welfare state' around Tring, and Hastoe Village Hall is amongst the endowments she bestowed. Designed by William Huckvale, it was built on the site of John Batchelor's Black Horse pub and brewery and William Wright's mill. The hall was opened in 1898 to serve as a community social and recreational centre in the midst of an area of the estate bounded by Tring, Wigginton, Buckland Common and Cholesbury.

For decades, Hastoe Men's Club flourished at the hall, providing billiards, skittles and other games for local farm and mill workers, and a well-stocked lending library was provided for the villagers' edification. With the benefit of the hall's stage and ample space, concerts and pantomimes were regularly presented.

In 1938 most of the local Rothschild estate was sold at auction, but the hall was retained with the intention of putting it in trust. The necessary legal work was overtaken by the Second World War and it was not until 1964 that the status of the hall was clarified by the execution of a trust deed. The Hastoe Village Hall Trust became a registered charity in September 2007.

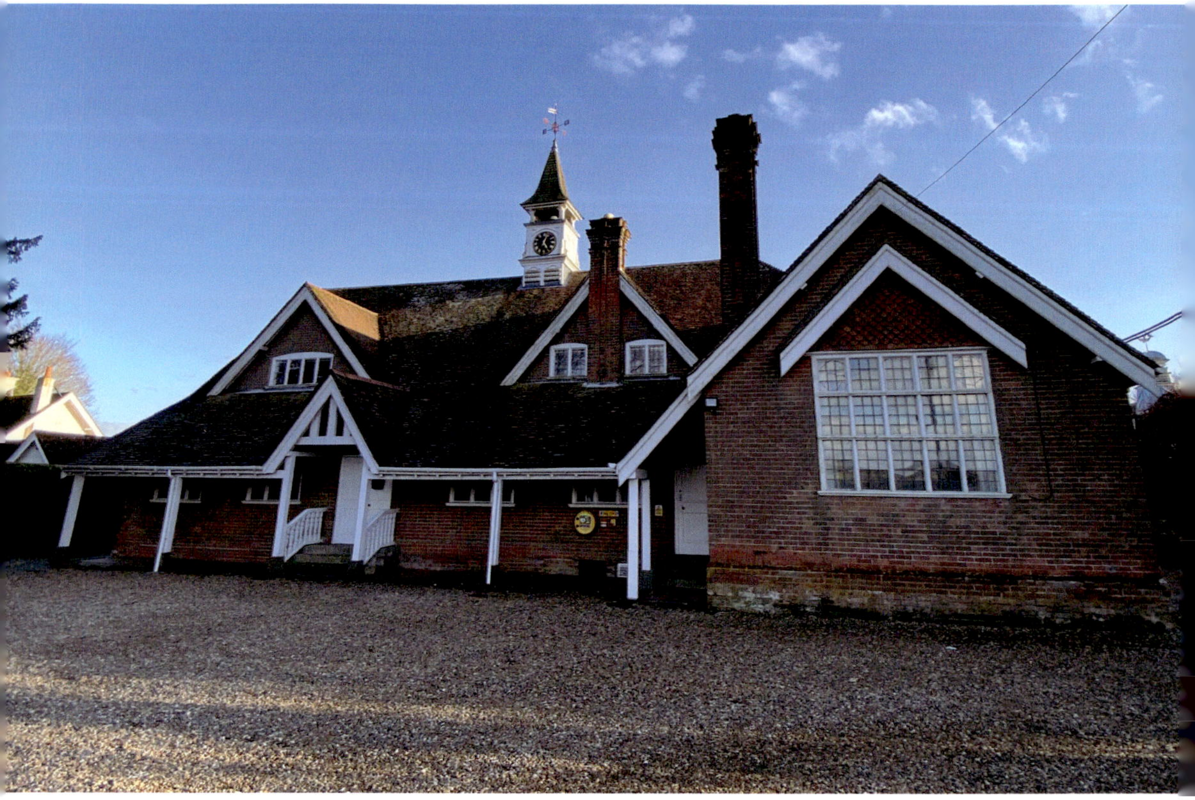

Hastoe Village Hall.

On the initiative of the Hall Management Committee and with support from The Hastoe Club and Residents' Association, the much-needed restoration of Hastoe Village Hall started in mid-2010. The aim was to restore the hall to the high standard of community resource envisaged when Lady Rothschild opened the hall in the 1890s and to enable the extent and variety of use of its original purpose.

After two years' effort, the hall was reopened on 25 November 2012 by Lord and Lady Rothschild.

27. Former Cattle Market Buildings, Brook Street

Tring Market, on Brook Street, was built by Lord Rothschild in 1893. Livestock had certainly been traded in Tring since the fourteenth century, having been present in the High Street, called 'Market Street' at the time. The market was run initially by Messrs W. Brown & Co., and later by their successors Brown and Merry, the estate agents and auctioneers. Livestock sales are no longer held here, with buildings converted for the sale of general goods and fine art. The former market office was designed by Huckvale, and is a fine red brick, three gabled half-timbered building, was converted in 2008 by Robert Tucker Associates as Tring Local History Museum, with the help of the Heritage Lottery Fund.

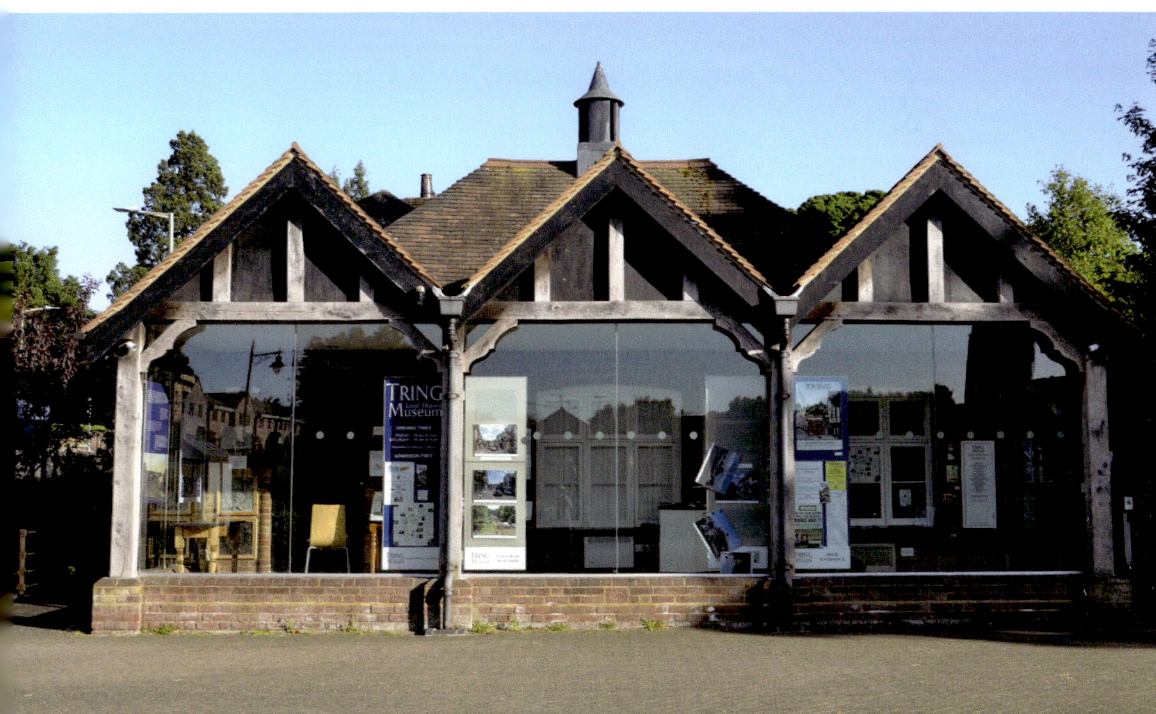

The old market office, now Tring Local History Museum.

28. Marshcroft Lane

Along Marshcroft Lane are a number of buildings of interest, which belonged to Pendley Manor. The Manor of Pendley had been purchased by Revd James Williams in 1864, a member of a Norfolk family who had made a fortune in the silk trade. At that time he was renting and residing at Tring Park mansion prior to its acquisition by the Rothschilds in 1872. A small part of the copyhold of the Manor of Pendley included an area on the south side of Tring Grove. Once the Williams family was living in their newly constructed house at Pendley, some attractive pairs of estate houses with decorative windows, porches, and tile hanging, as well as a laundry building to serve this big house, were erected on this land in Marshcroft Lane.

Halfway down the lane at Marshcroft itself, two houses had been erected by the Rothschild Estate in 1881 on the site of earlier cottages (on the front of these properties square frames of brickwork still outline the position of the original plaques which bore the Rothschild coat of arms). The occupants comprised a farm carter, his wife and five children, and next door lived a shepherd, wife and four children. In 1890 these properties and Park Hill Farm were the subject of a land exchange between Lord Rothschild and J. G. Williams, and at a later stage they were bequeathed to Dorian Williams by his aunt.

Marshcroft Lane, former Pendley Estate buildings.

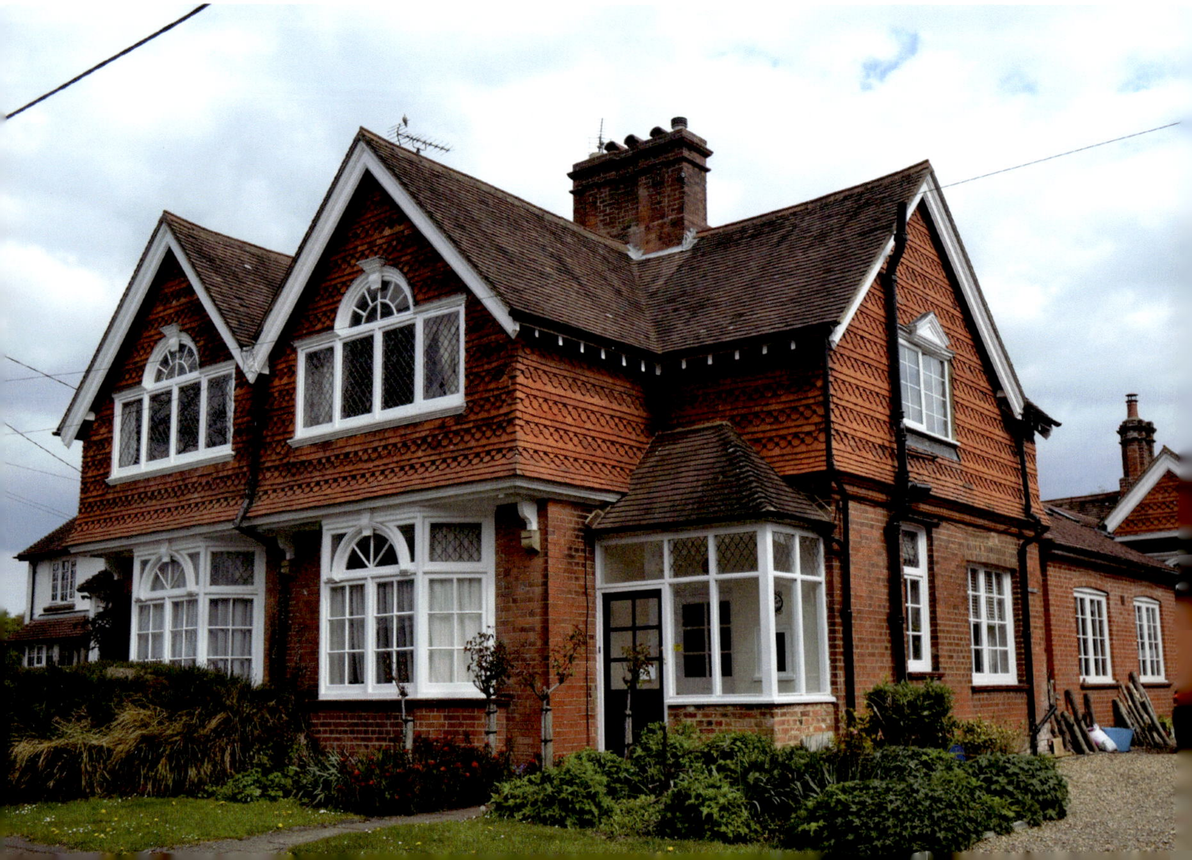

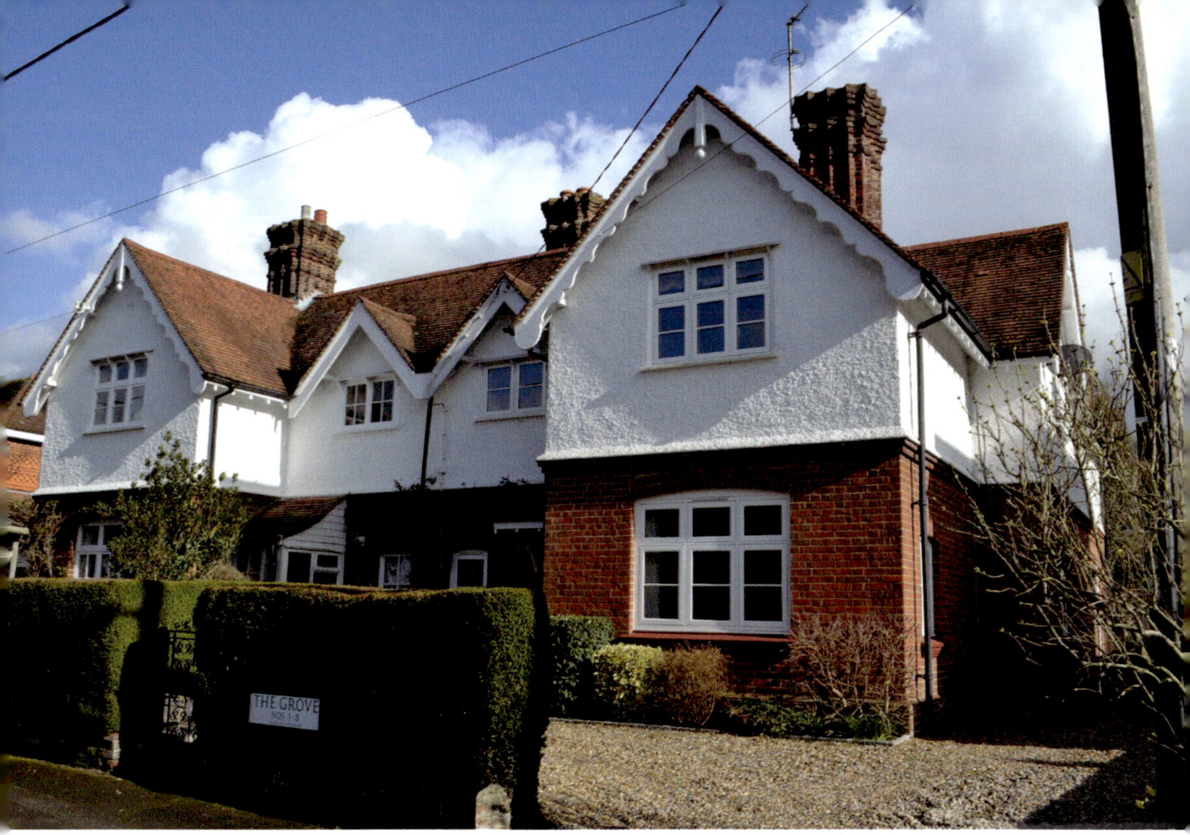

Marshcroft Lane.

Park Hill Farm, so called from the old medieval field name and now known as Marshcroft Farm, stands at the end of the lane between the Grand Union Canal and the railway line. For many years it was held by Joseph Clarke, a tenant of the Rothschilds. The farmhouse has been converted to one private dwelling, as has a very large old granary nearby.

29. Former Post Office, High Street

No. 69 High Street was built as the Post Office in 1883. The *Bucks Herald* wrote on 7 July 1883, 'The New Post Office. On Tuesday last, the postal business of Tring was transferred to the new premises. The Office, a spacious room, fifty-five feet in length, thirty-feet in breath [sic], and of proportionate height, contains fittings of the most approved construction as regards utility, providing accommodation for the Parcels Post, and for the eleven town and rural letter carriers at present employed, whilst the ample space apportioned to the telegraph instruments is in striking contrast to the crowded state of the telegraph branch in the old office. The building is in the domestic Gothic style of the sixteenth century, sufficiently modified to furnish the light and ventilation specially required in the post office. The architect, Mr. W. Huckvale, and the builders, Messrs. James Honour and Son, may be congratulated on the result of their efforts.' The postmaster at the time was Mr William Rodwell, with deliveries four times each weekday. Today it is a popular restaurant.

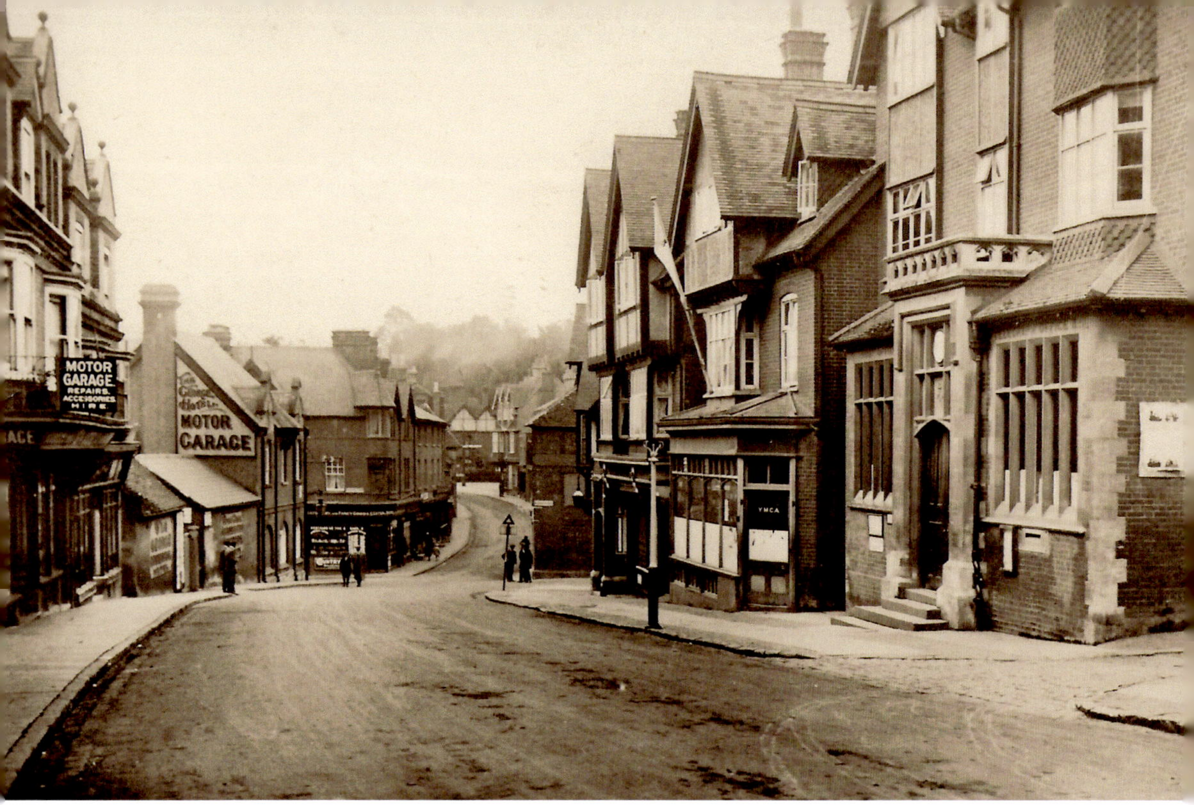

Above: The High Street with the old post office on the right-hand side of the street.

Below: The former post office, now a restaurant.

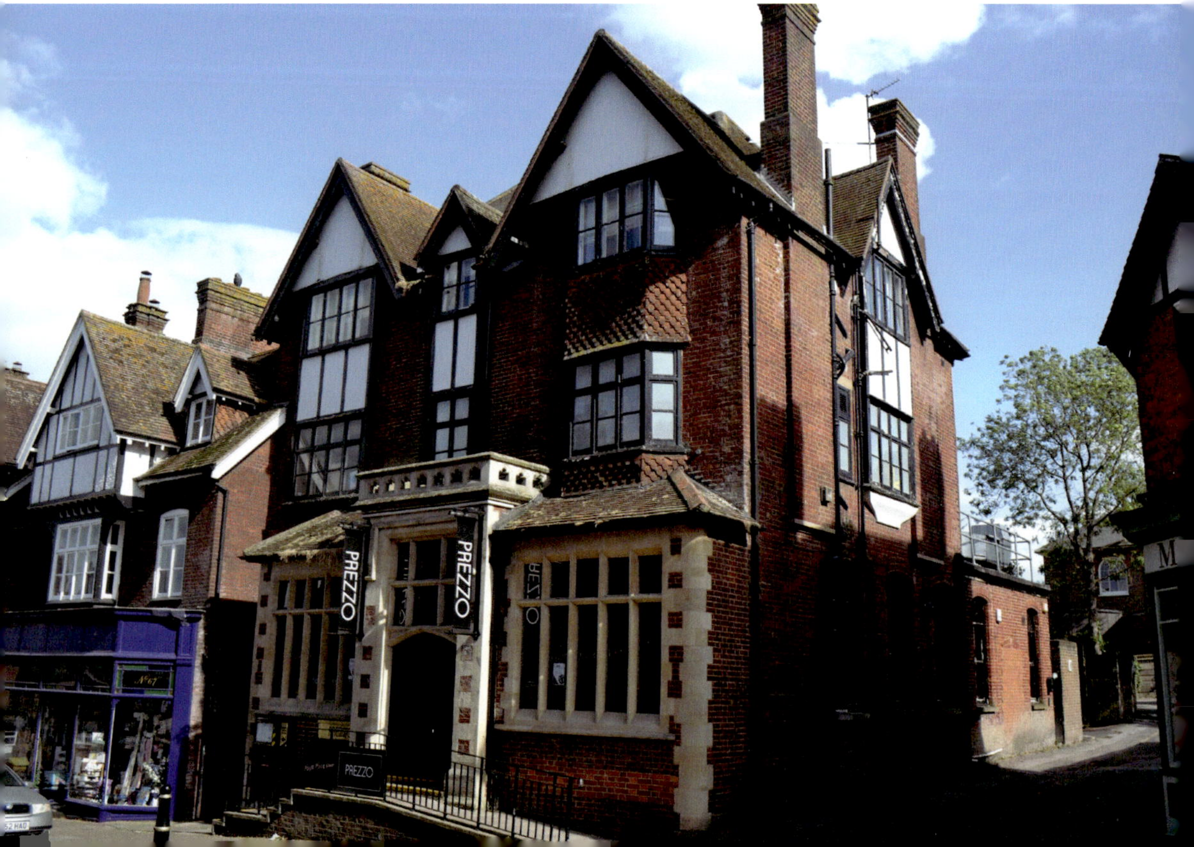

30. Victoria Hall, Akeman Street

The appearance of Akeman Street today is predominantly nineteenth century. However, it was established as a street by the seventeenth century, and probably well before. It retains at least two buildings with sixteenth-century work, at Nos 12 and 15, which are the earliest structures known in the current conservation area, apart from the parish church and the tithe barn. It has other early buildings with timber framing and brick-nogging, steeply pitched tile roofs, and leaded casements, for example at Nos 13, 81, and 90, the first two having clasped purlin roofs, which suggest a date not later than the seventeenth century. However, the street was much rebuilt and refronted in the early nineteenth century, hence the predominance of late Georgian and Victorian architecture.

At the lower end of Akeman Street is the Victoria Hall, built on the site of the old Assembly Rooms, which dated from 1825, the current building constructed in 1886 as a purpose-built dance hall. The designer was William Huckvale, who designed it in the Italian Renaissance style, and it provides a rare example in Tring of a building with classical orders. Sadly it proved not profitable, and at the turn of the twentieth century was known as Victoria Works, with a firm manufacturing mineral water, cider, pickles and vinegar. This was short-lived and for many years it housed the town library. Today it is used for events, exhibitions and local meetings.

Victoria Hall, Akeman Street, designed by William Huckvale.

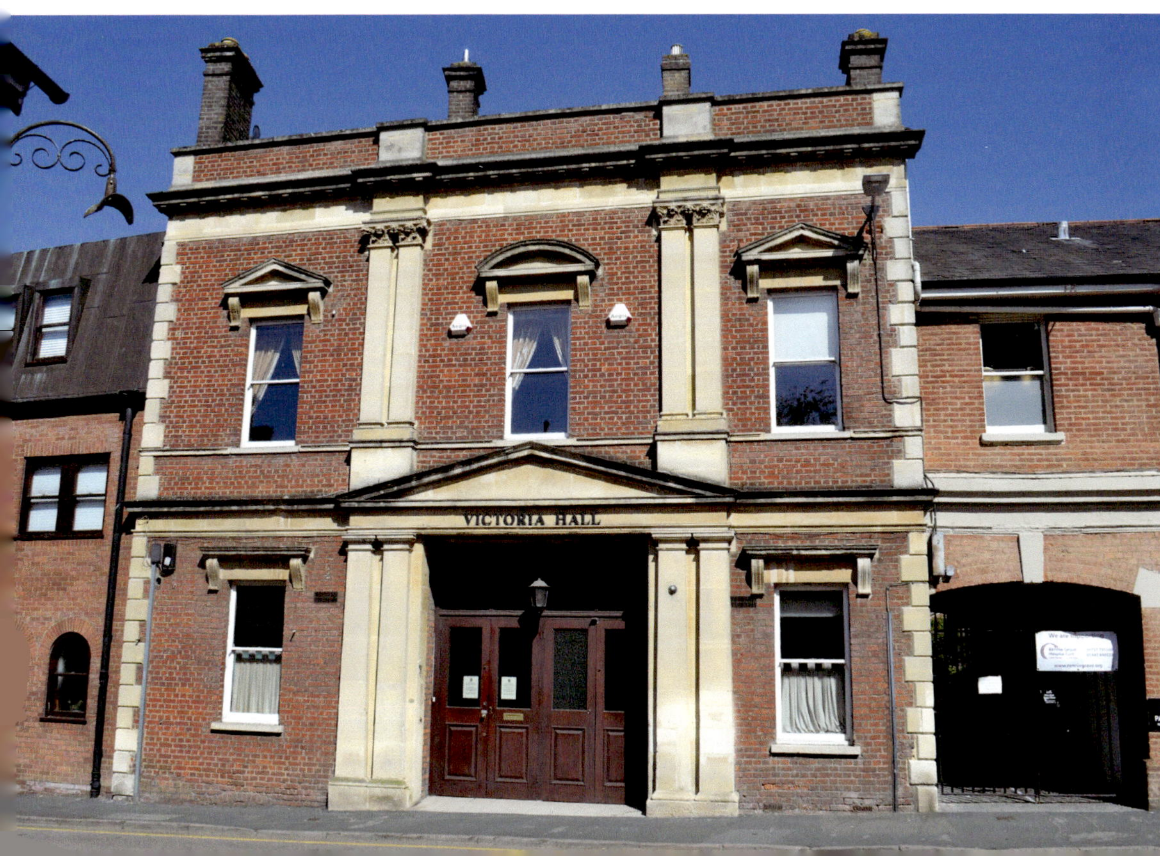

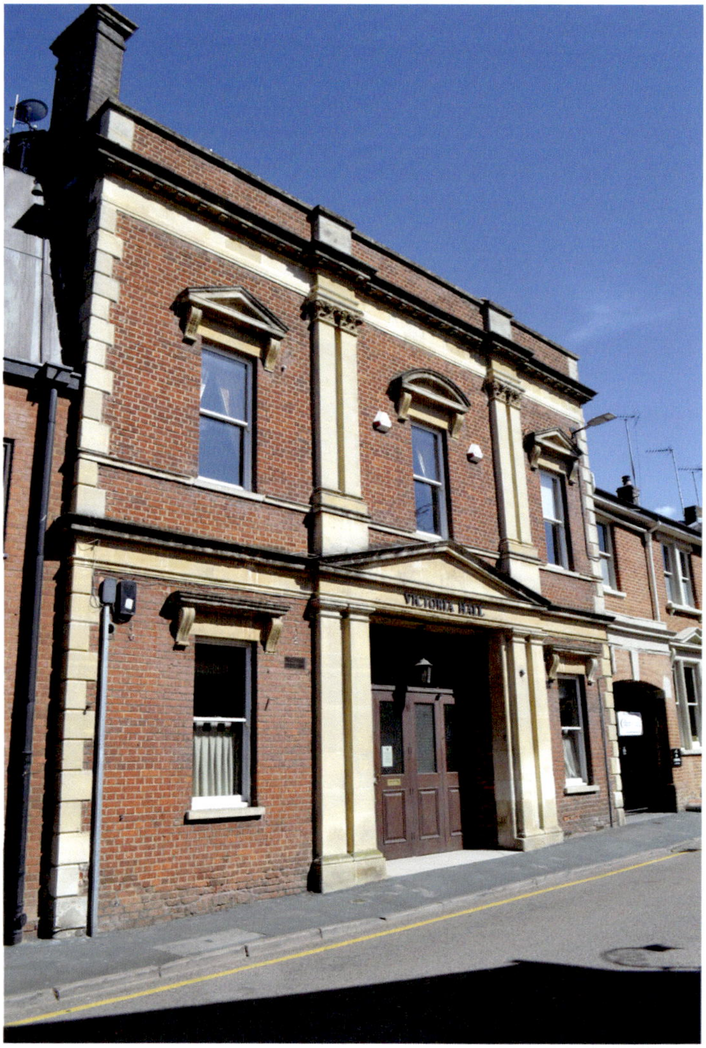

Victoria Hall, once a purpose-built dance hall but now a venue for a wide range of community uses.

31. Former Baptist Chapel, Frogmore Street, and New Baptist Church, High Street

This former Baptist chapel was one of the first to be built in Hertfordshire and was built at Frogmore End, now Frogmore Street, in 1751 and registered as a place of worship in 1801. It was unfortunately described as 'one of the queerest, stuffiest, ugliest little chapels you can conceive of. It has a graveyard in front which the road turns to avoid'. By the late 1830s it had been enlarged with a graveyard in front of it but eventually closed, becoming, for a time, an antiques shop and eventually converted to residential use.

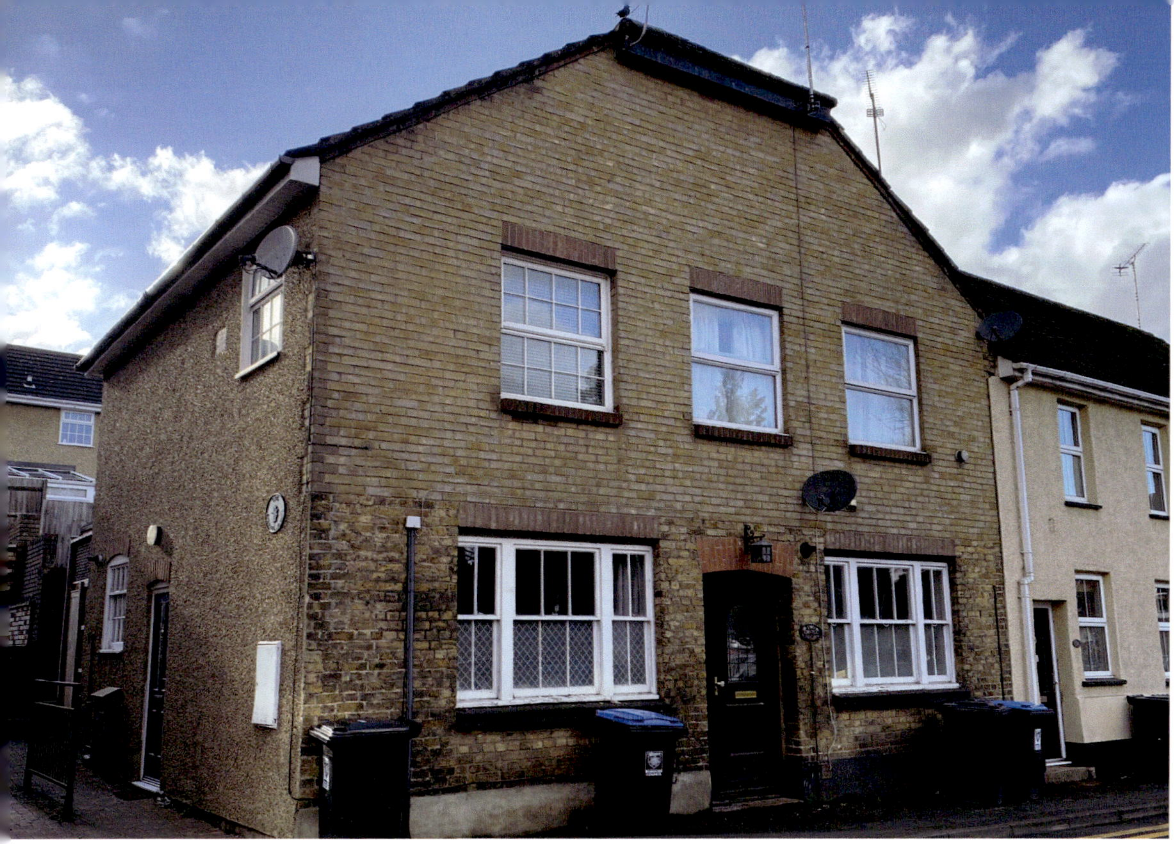

Above: The former Baptist chapel on Frogmore Street, now residential.

Below: The 'new' Baptist Church on the High Street, completed in 1889 to the designs of William Huckvale.

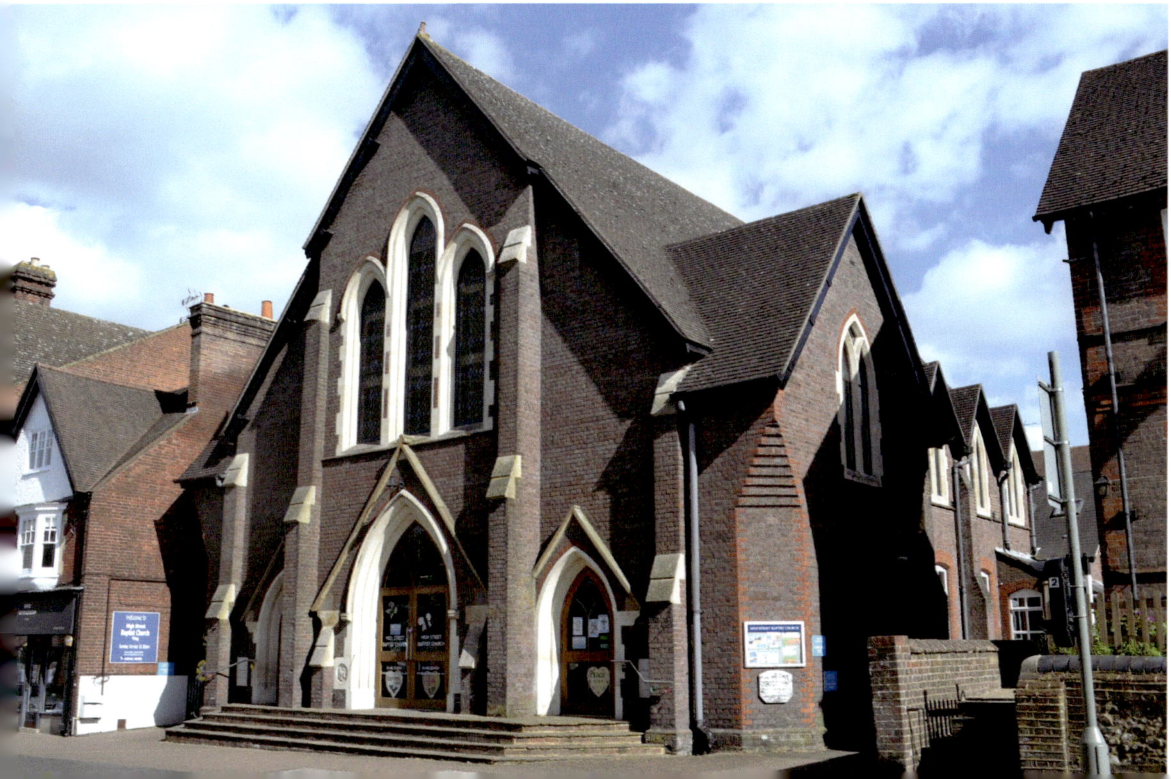

A new Baptist Church was built later in the nineteenth century in the High Street, by William Huckvale, described by Pevsner as 'very restrained'. It was completed in 1889 and comprised a church with a lecture hall. A new organ was bought in 1949 to replace the one that had been there since the beginning of the century.

32. Tring Zoological Museum

The Natural History Museum at Tring was once the private museum of Lionel Walter, 2nd Baron Rothschild, and is located in the grounds of the former Rothschild family home of Tring Park. Built to the designs of William Huckvale by the 1st Baron Rothschild as a twenty-first birthday present to Lionel in 1889, it housed his collection of mounted specimens and was first opened to the public in 1892. He left the museum and its contents to the nation in 1937. Lionel Walter bred hybrids between zebras and horses (zebroids) and a hybrid foal is on display. He was frequently seen riding a zebra-drawn carriage. The museum's Zebra café alludes to Lord Rothschild's love of zebras and has photographs of his trained zebras harnessed to open carriages.

As the collection grew, by 1911 the museum was too small to house all its possessions, including birds, animals and insects. That year, an extension was constructed with further space for exhibitions, workrooms and a study for Walter, which remains intact. When Walter died on 27 August 1937 at nearby Home Farm, it was given to the nation and taken over by the Natural History Museum

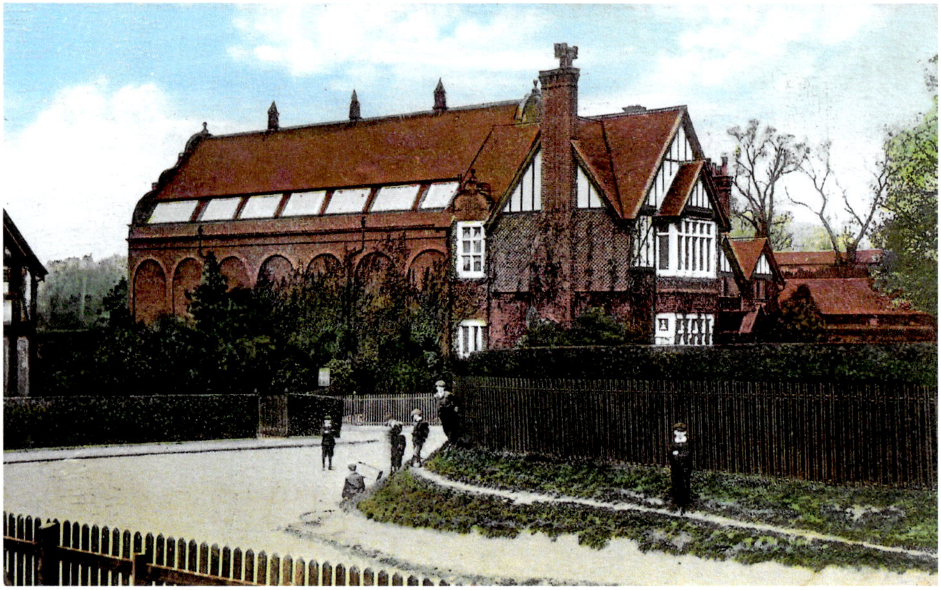

An early view of Tring Museum.

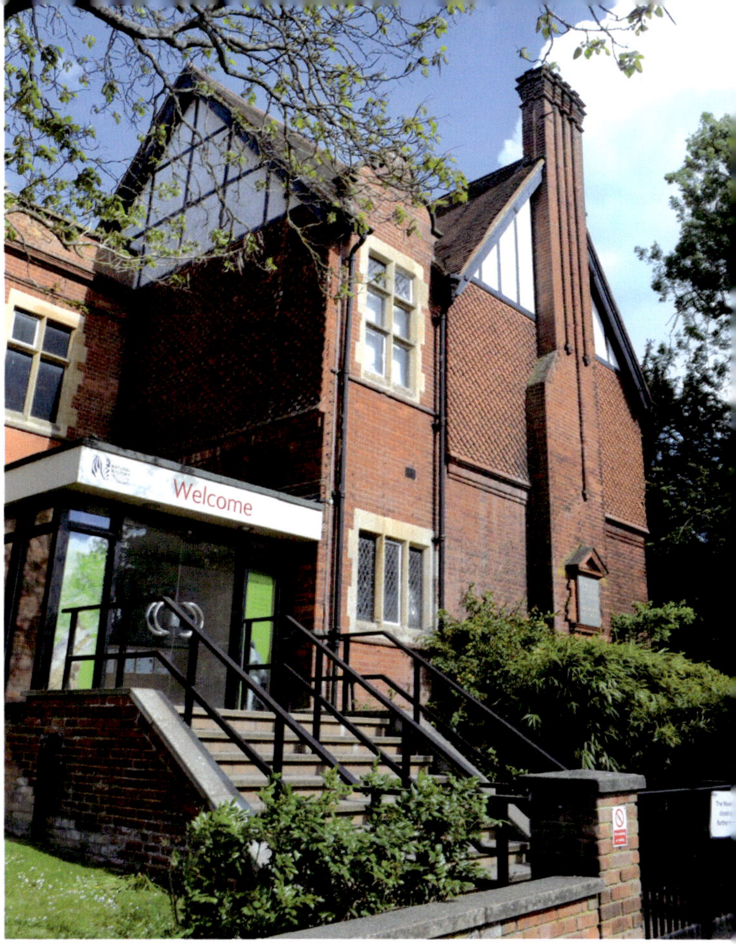

Right: Architect William Huckvale was Rothschild's preferred architect.

Below: The museum extension, built in 1911 to house the growing collection.

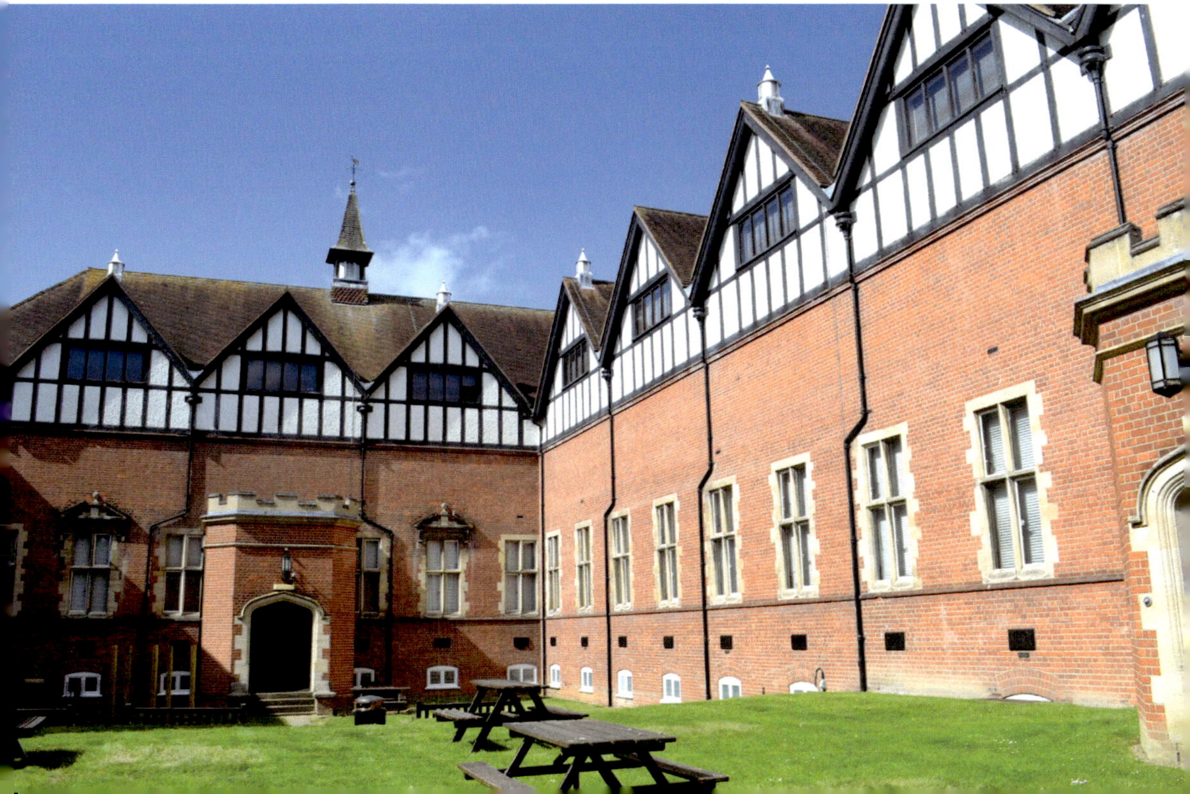

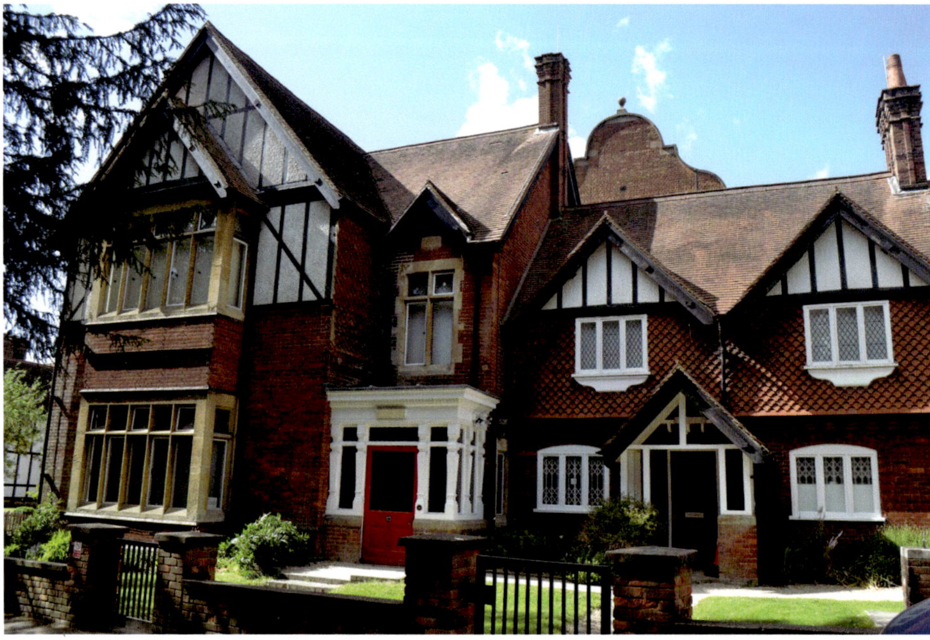

The cottage above and on the right-hand side was the home of Alfred Minall, who was Walter Rothschild's taxidermist. Walter always dreamed of having his own museum and in 1880 he made Alfred Minall his curator.

in London, who stated that the collection was 'of great scientific interest, especially the butterflies and insects'.

The site of Walter Rothschild's Zoological Museum is also home to the ornithological research collections (Bird Group, Department of Zoology) and the ornithological library of the Natural History Museum. These collections are probably the largest and most comprehensive in the world, with over 2 million skin, skeleton, spirit, egg and nest specimens, representing over 95 per cent of known bird species, housed adjacent to one of the world's great ornithological libraries.

33. Constitutional Club/Conservative Club

The Tring and District Conservative Club, in Western Road, is a structure of red brick with stone dressings, erected in 1892, at the expense of Joseph Grout Williams Esq. JP of Pendley Manor, and comprised a reading room, lounge, two billiard rooms, a committee room and offices. The Constitutional Club closed in early 1924 after the death of Williams, who was a major patron and friend of the club, but reopened as the Conservative Club on 10 May the same year, with the first President Major Vivian Williams, heir to the Pendley estate.

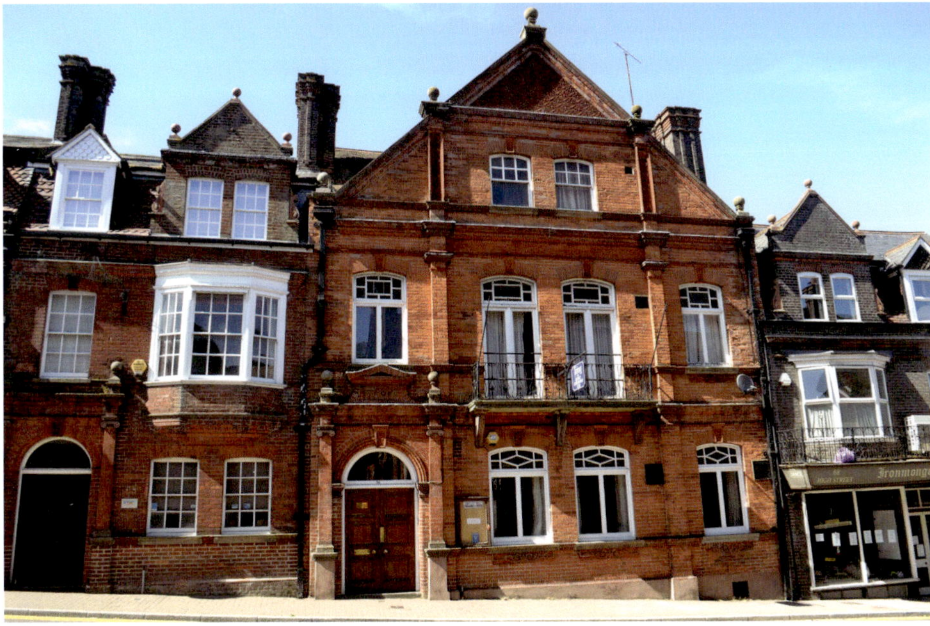

Above: The former Constitutional Club, now Conservative Club.

Below: Erected in 1892 and funded by J. G. Williams of Pendley Manor.

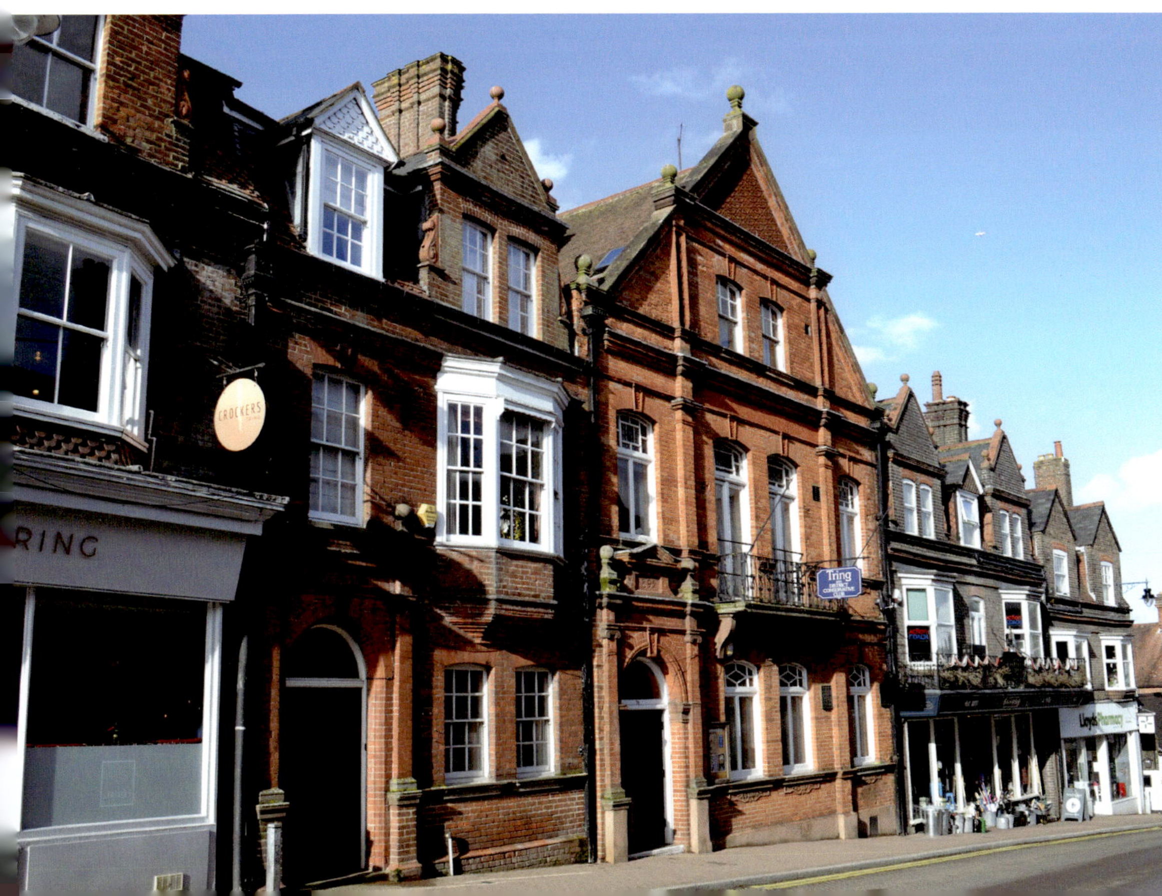

34. Louisa Cottages

Described by Pevsner as 'rather spiky vernacular style', on the corner of Akeman Street and Park Road are the almshouses, commonly known as Louisa Cottages. Nos 1–5 are dated 1893, whilst Nos 6–8 are dated 1901. These beautiful cottages were designed by William Huckvale in the Tudoresque style for the Rothschild

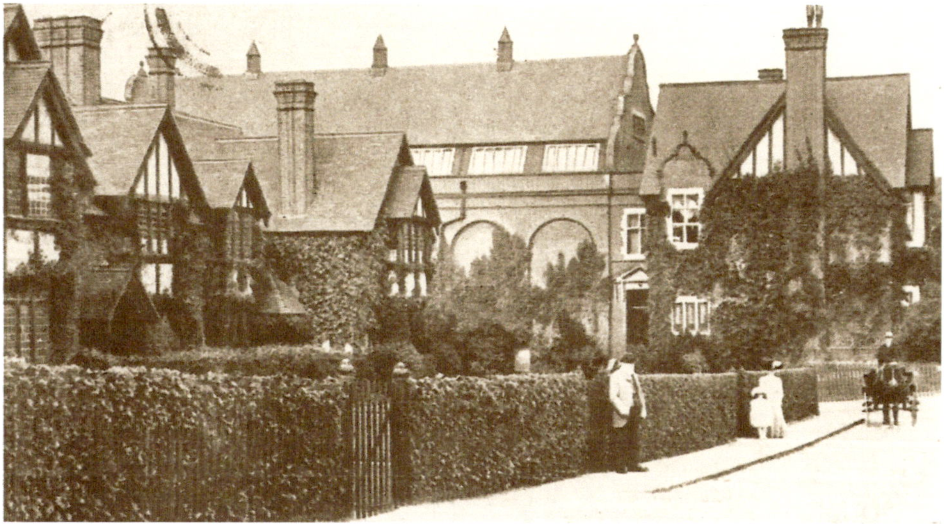

Above: Louisa Cottages with the museum in the background.

Below: The Tudor vernacular of the cottages, described by Pevsner as 'spiky'.

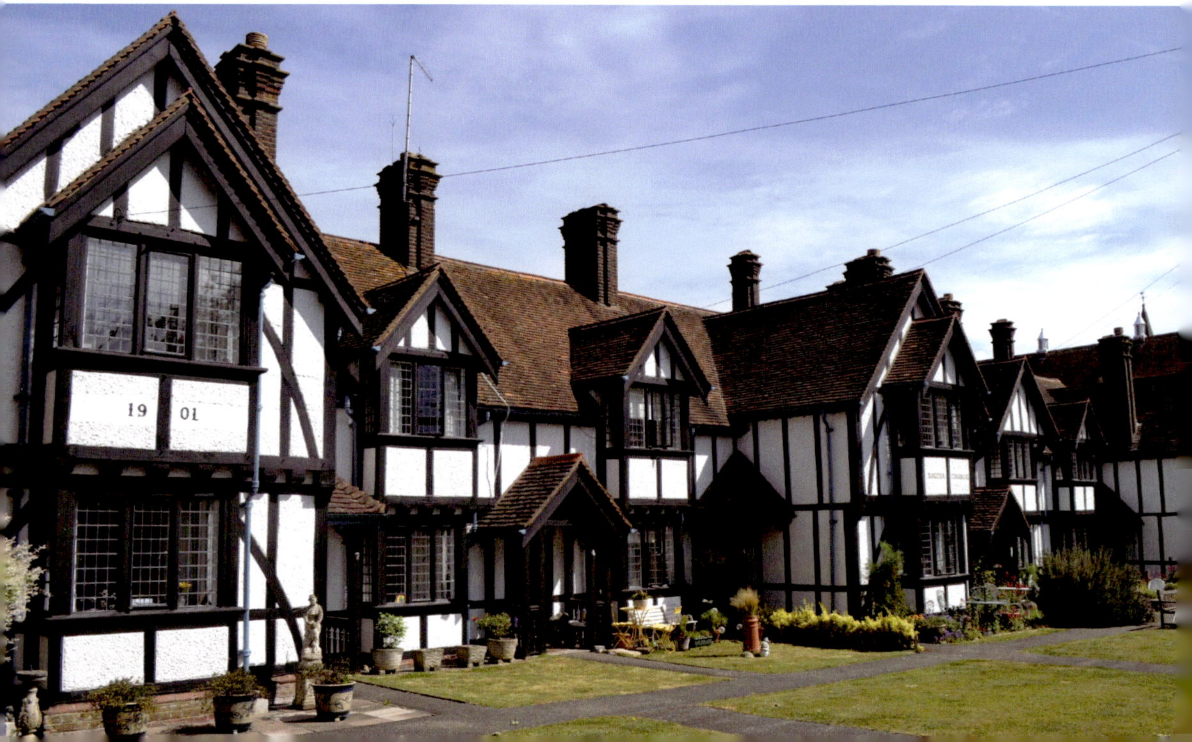

estate, specifically as almshouses for retired workers. They were the brainchild of Emma Rothschild in memory of her mother, Louisa.

The Rothschild family had a major influence on Tring and the local population when they moved here in 1872. In particular, Nathaniel and Emma Rothschild brought the town and its residents many significant changes. Nathaniel was responsible for clearing away slum houses off Akeman Street and Frogmore Street and built fifty modern cottages which were presented to the town council. Many cottages on the Tring Estate were also rebuilt.

Other improvements they were responsible for included supporting local industries, building an isolation hospital, founding the Chiltern Hills Spring Water Company, and organising a health service for the town. The Louisa Cottages are a reminder of their philanthropic contribution to the town.

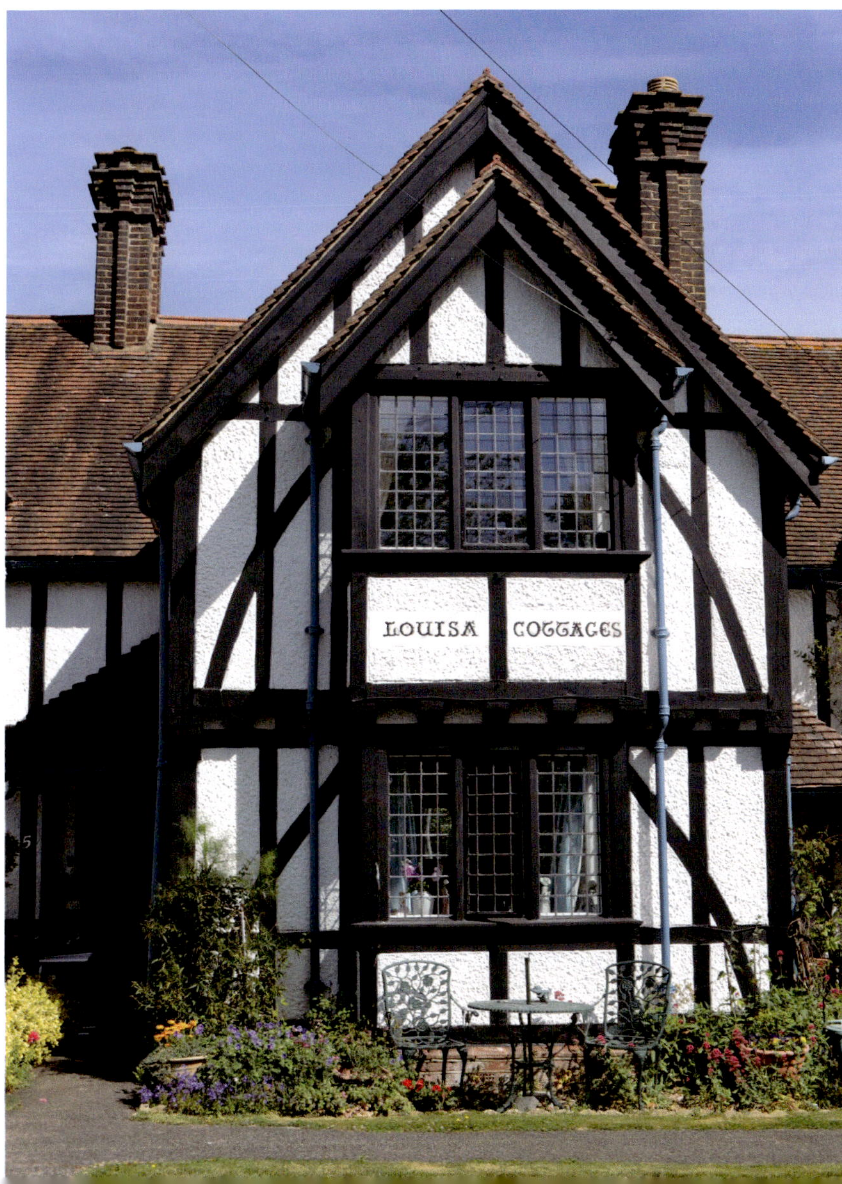

Louisa Cottages today.

35. Tring Cemetery

The inclusion of Tring Cemetery is important as it contains a chapel and gate lodge and is approached on Western Road, noted for its fine nineteenth- and twentieth-century Victorian villas. The cemetery is also considered a park and garden of local historic interest and is described by the Hertfordshire Gardens Trust (2010) as 'an unspoiled Victorian cemetery with picturesque chapel and lodge, Tring Cemetery was laid out in 1891–3 just north of the Aylesbury road at the very edge of the town. Most of the land was gifted by Nathaniel Mayer Rothschild of Tring Park. The lodge at the entrance by the main road is in neo-Elizabethan style with flint and brick walls, inside wrought iron gates. The drive curves uphill to the chapel, which is of flint with brick angle-buttresses and stone window dressings, and has a Tudor-style polygonal chimney in brick. The chapel and the layout were designed by William Huckvale, retained by the Rothschild family, whose head gardener advised on the planting. Much of this survives, the southern (consecrated) section with its curving avenue being different in style to the northern unconsecrated section for Nonconformists, which has a square path.'

The picturesque chapel in Tring Cemetery.

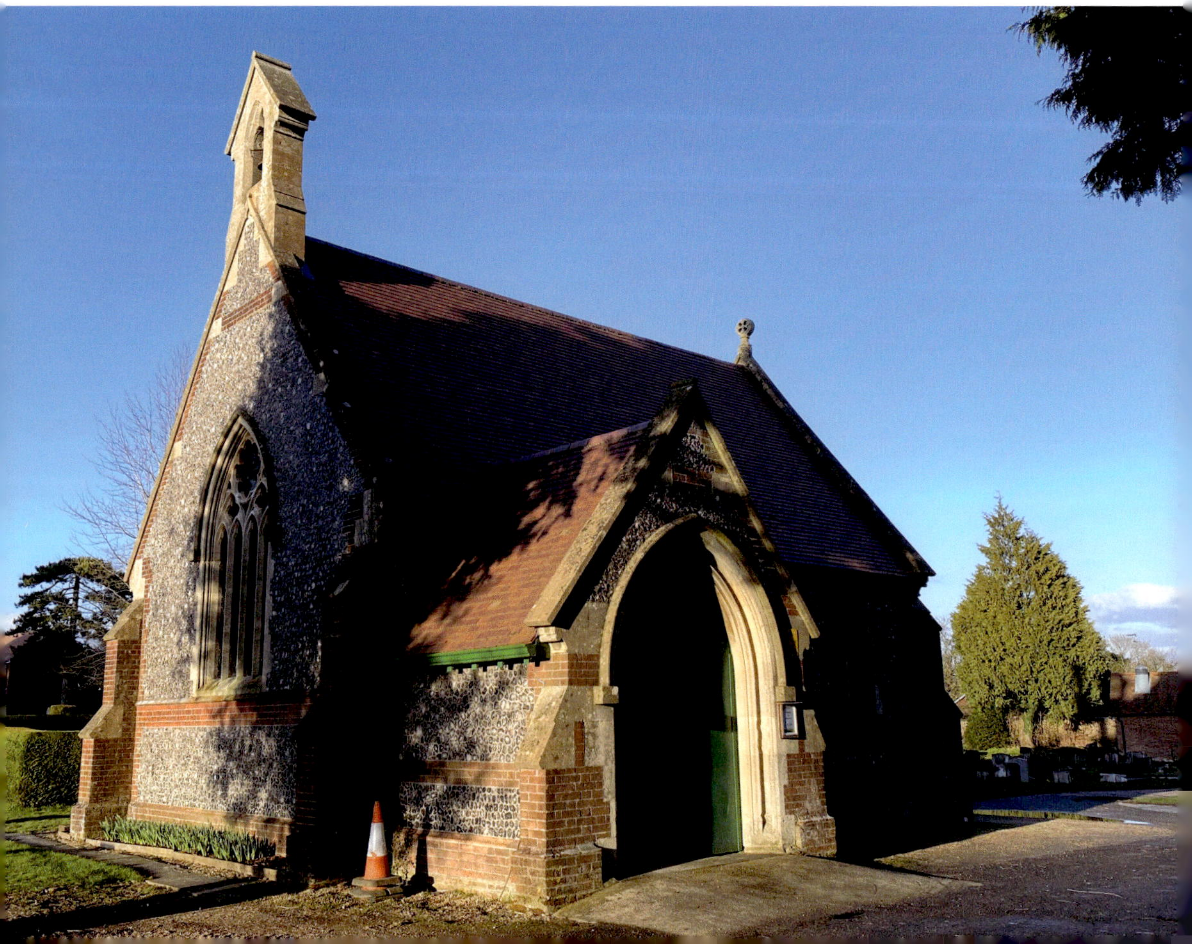

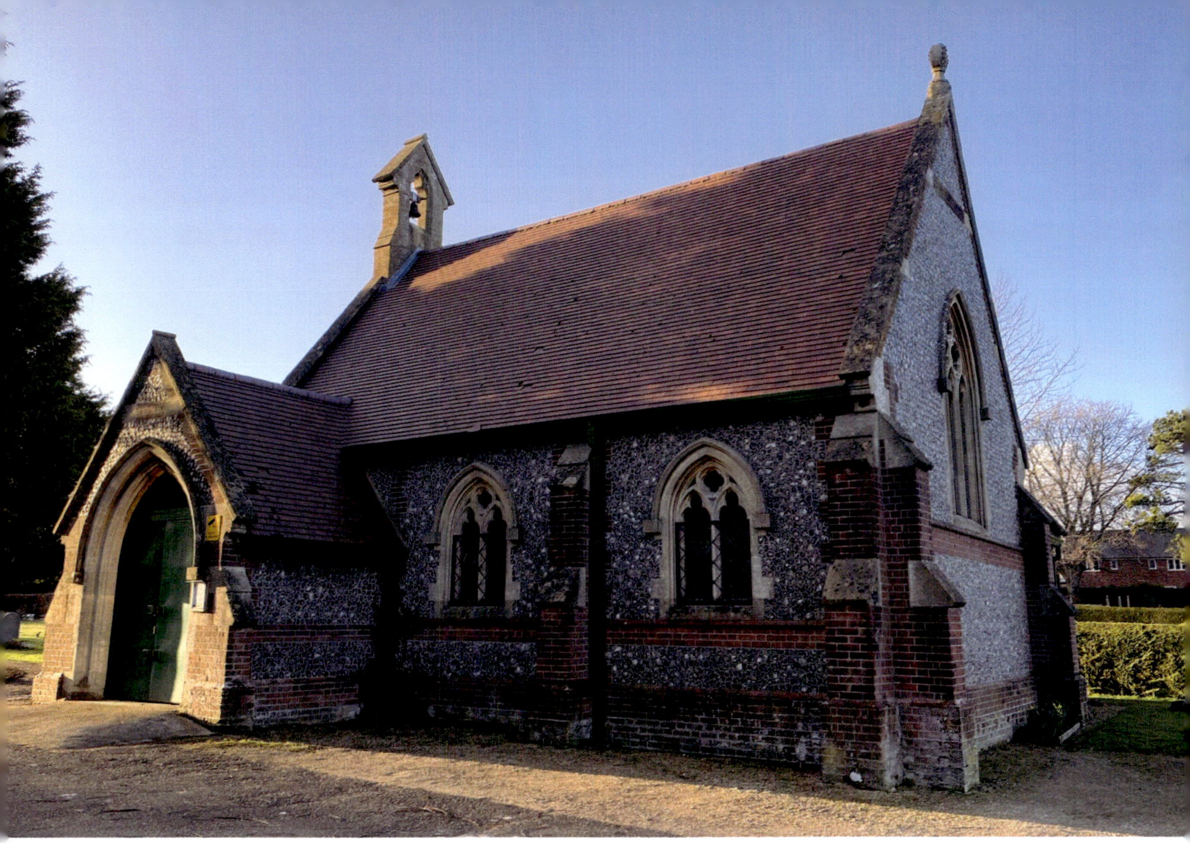

Above: Designed by William Huckvale between 1891 and 1893.

Below: The cemetery lodge by the main entrance.

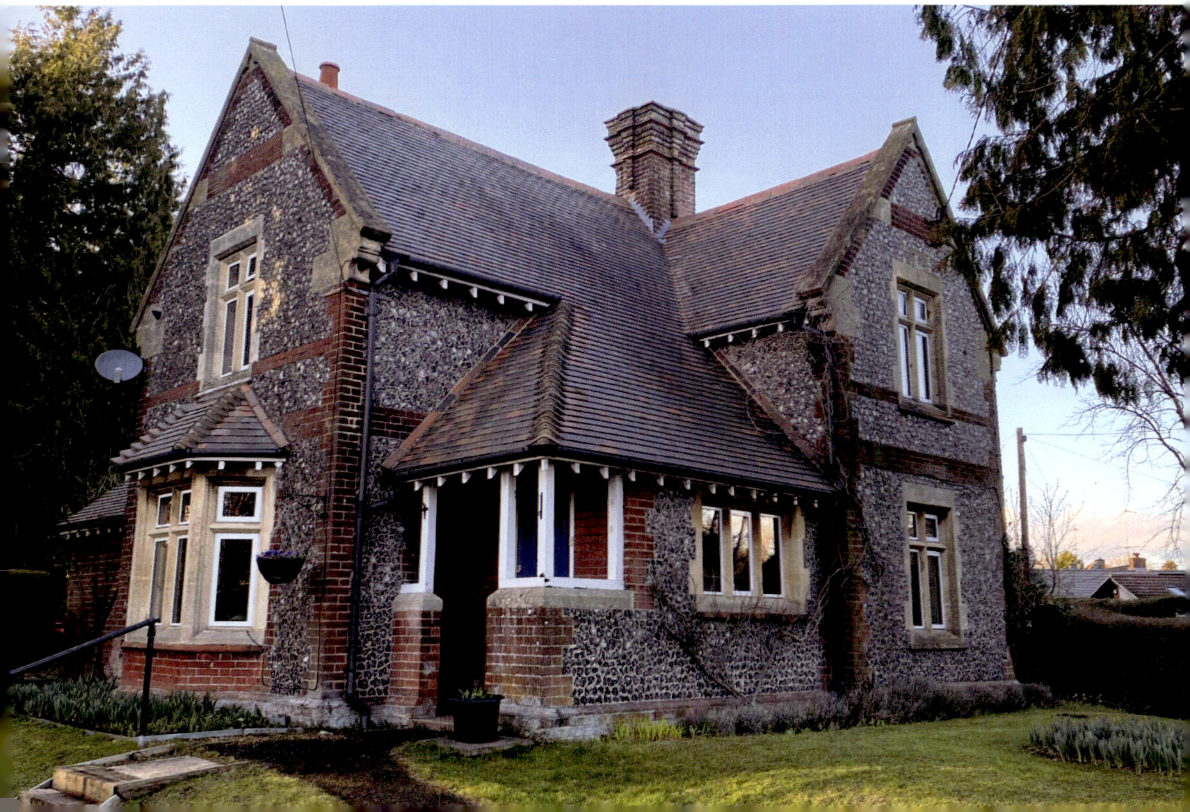

36. Home Farm

Home Farm formed a key part of the Rothschild estate; it is also where Walter Rothschild died in 1937. During the Second World War, it was used as a maternity home run by volunteers. After the war it was sold to Flight-Lieutenant Kilby, who made a number of additions, including an ornamental pool with a fountain and two life-size female figures, all built in the centre of the farmyard. Under the

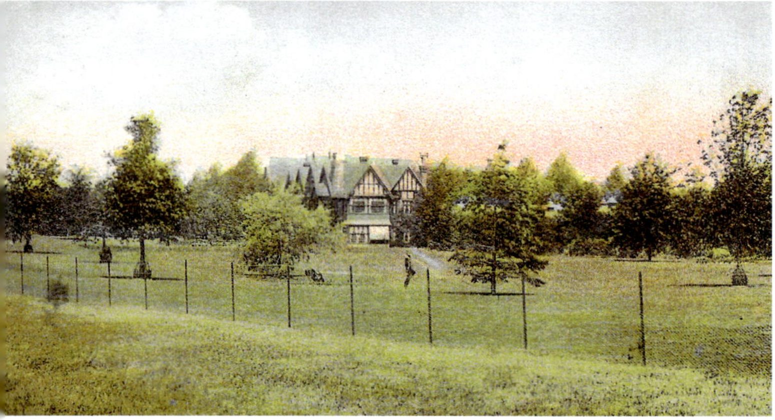

Left: An early view of Home Farm.

Below: Home Farm, where Walter Rothschild died in 1937.

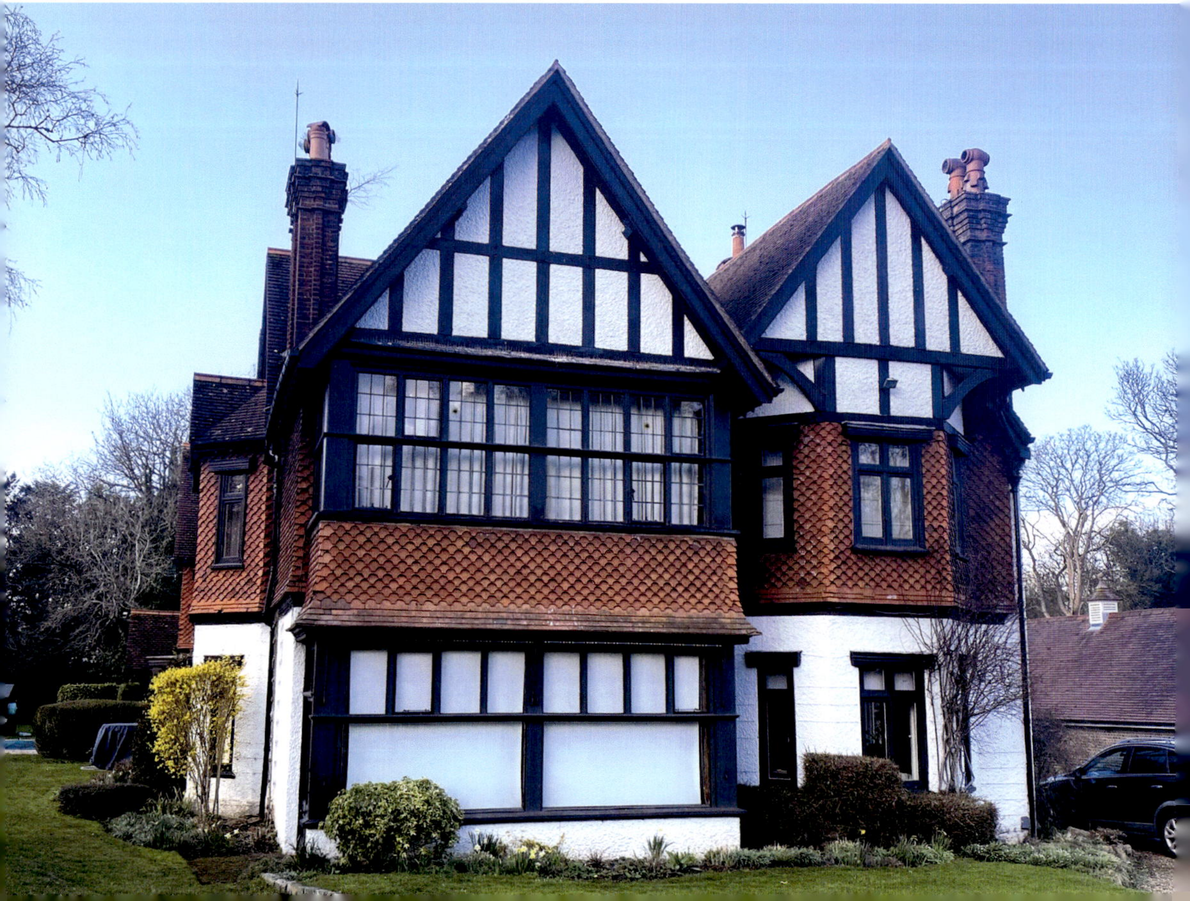

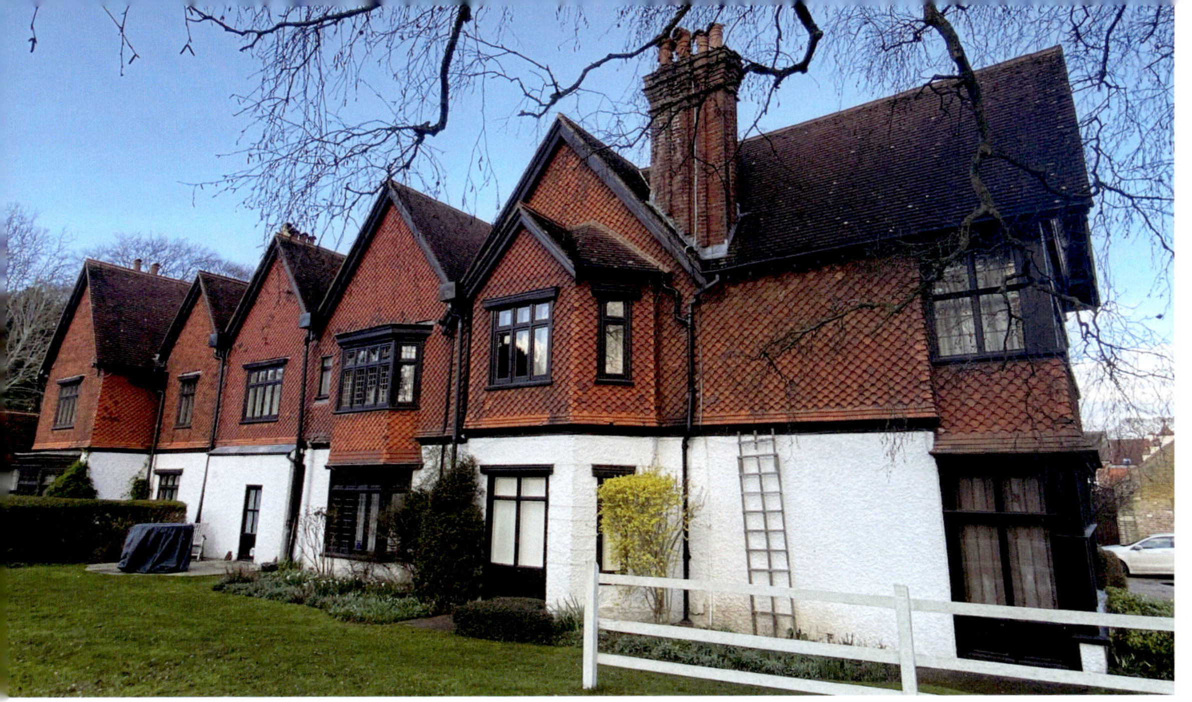

Above: Home Farm served as a maternity home run by volunteers during the Second World War.

Right: Home Farm, from Carr's Drive.

Below: Buildings of Home Farm, now residential.

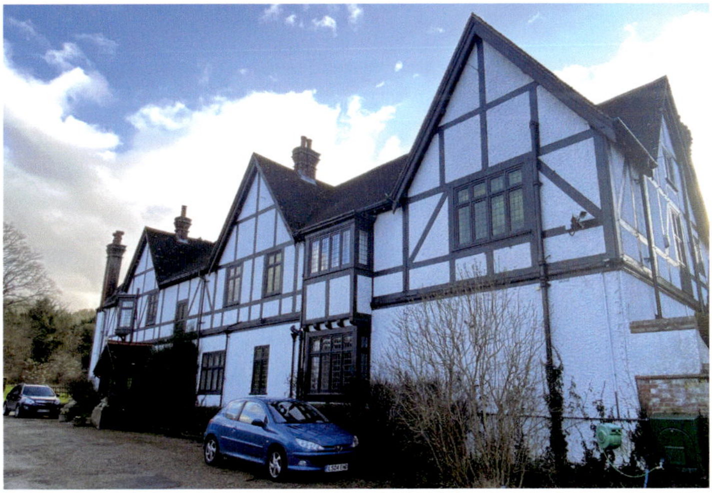

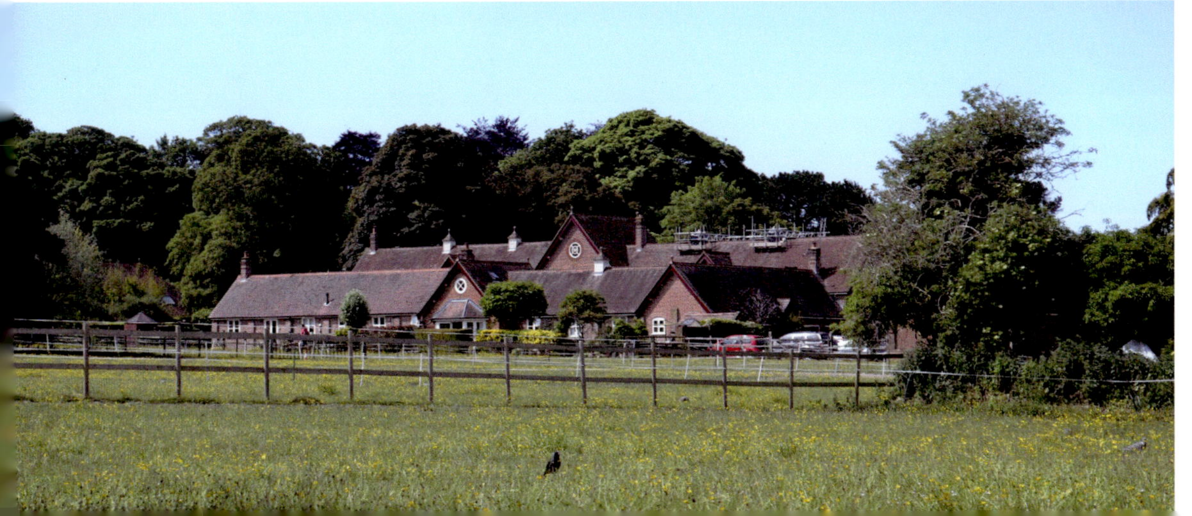

name White Cloud Farm, it eventually became the home of the Moss family, with Stirling Moss becoming a world-champion racing driver in the 1960s. The road to the house is called Carr's Drive, after Richardson Carr, who was the agent for the estate and the occupant of Home Farm. The census of 1891 lists him, aged thirty-four years old, with his wife Mary, daughter Catherine and three servants.

The extensive ranges of farm buildings have now been converted into private houses.

37. The Manse, Grove Road

On a slightly elevated plot at the far end of Grove Road on the east side near New Mill stands a detached house which was built to serve as the manse for the nearby Baptist Church in New Road. Erected in 1894, it was a gift from the Mead family, who owned the flour mill, now Heygates, and in the census of 1901 is named Hilldene Villa. This property, except for brief periods when it has been rented out,

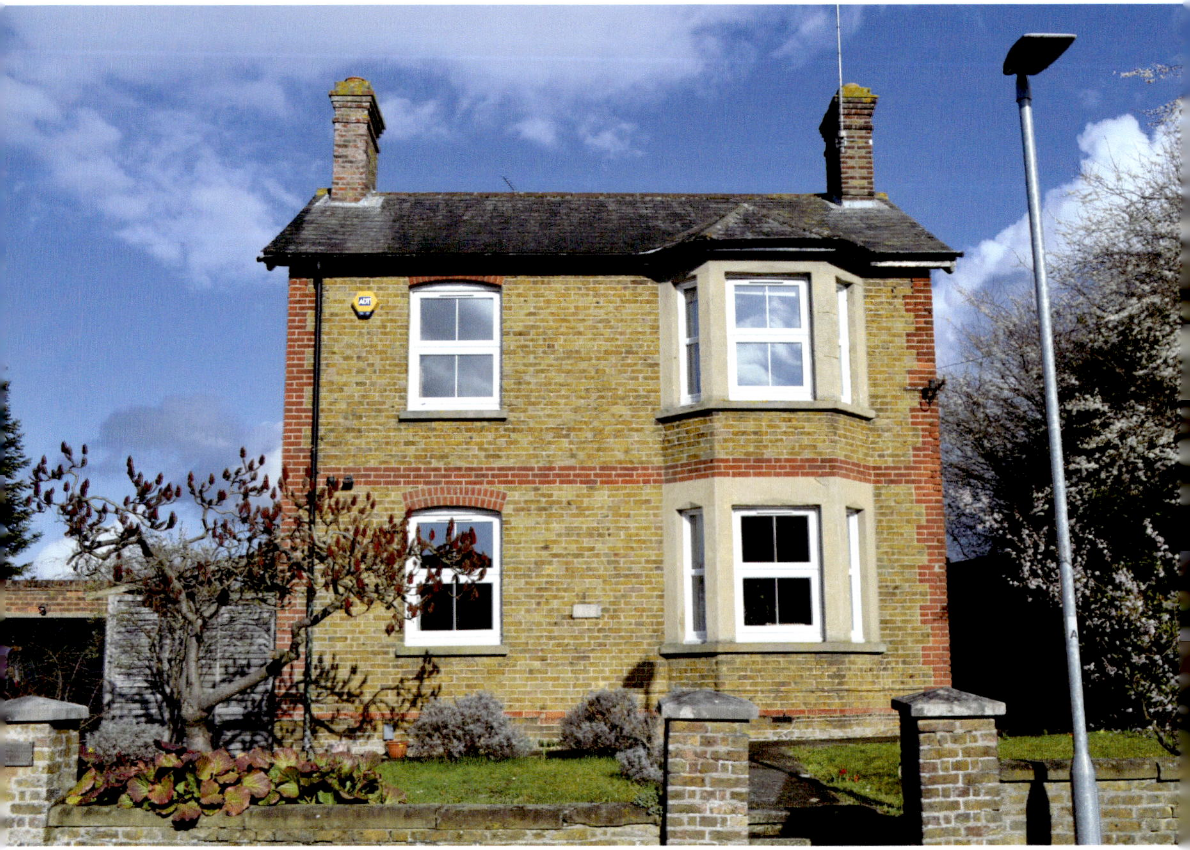

The Manse, home to Baptist ministers for many years.

has been in continuous occupation by ministers of the Baptist Church. Baptist origins in the local area started in New Mill, where John Bunyan on his travels is said to have 'preached in the fields' – hence the name of the modern Bunyan Close on the west side of Grove Road.

38. Ardenoak House

At the end of this western section of High Street is Ardenoak House, No. 101. It is a late Georgian villa of similar style to the houses on Akeman Street, although of larger size and a higher social status. It has a double-pile plan with lateral chimney stacks and a classical porch with orders and fan light. Formerly Elm House, it was long a private residence, but also housed a girls' school in the early twentieth century, run by the Misses Daisy, Frances and Lily Collins. When built it was in the country on the outskirts of the town.

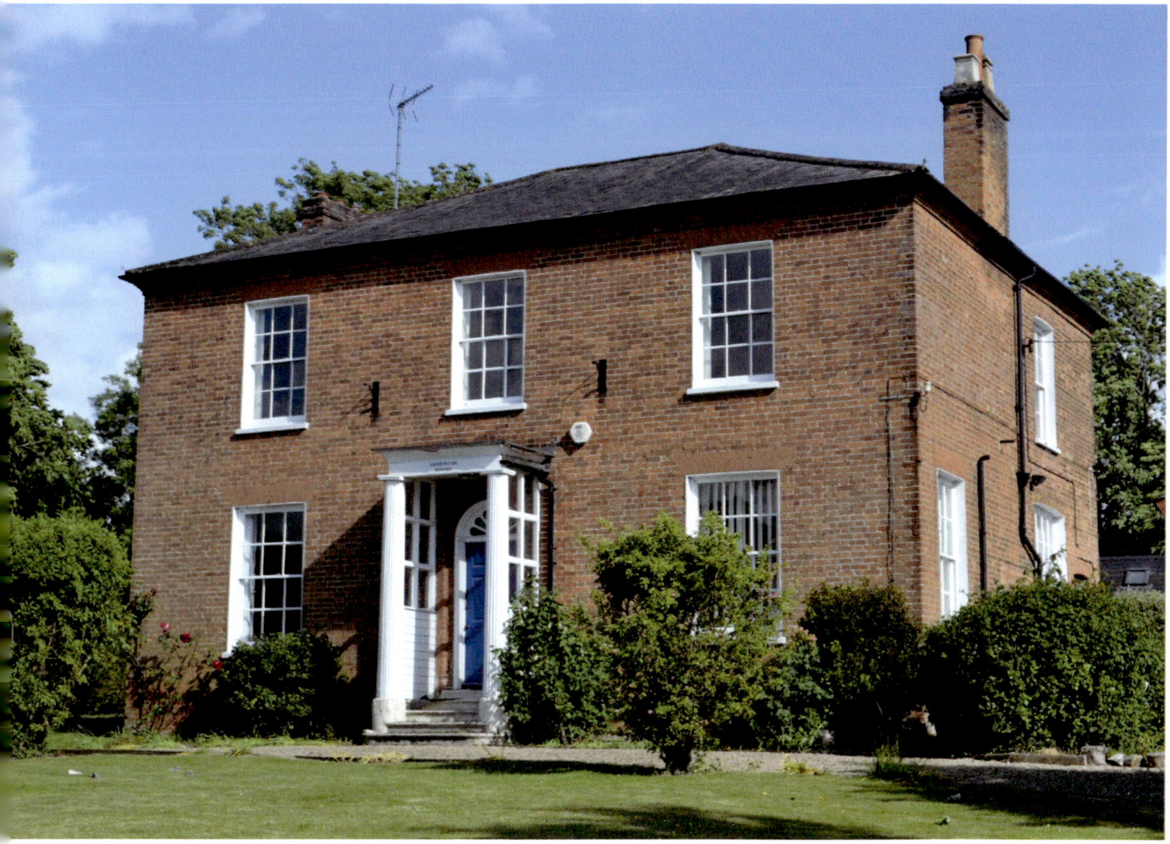

Ardenoak House, once known as Elm House, was for a time the home and surgery of Dr Le Quesne. His carriage and coachman were well known throughout the town and surrounding villages.

39. The Old Church House

The Old Church House was built in the sixtieth year of Queen Victoria's reign by public subscription for the parish church – completed in 1896. It was used as a church and community hall until the 1970s. It is also said to have housed the Tring Library for a short time. The parish church eventually gave up its use and it was purchased by the Tring Youth Club, receiving support from the County Council Youth Dept. When running a youth club on the site became no longer tenable during the late 1980s the hall was placed in trust for the youth of the town.

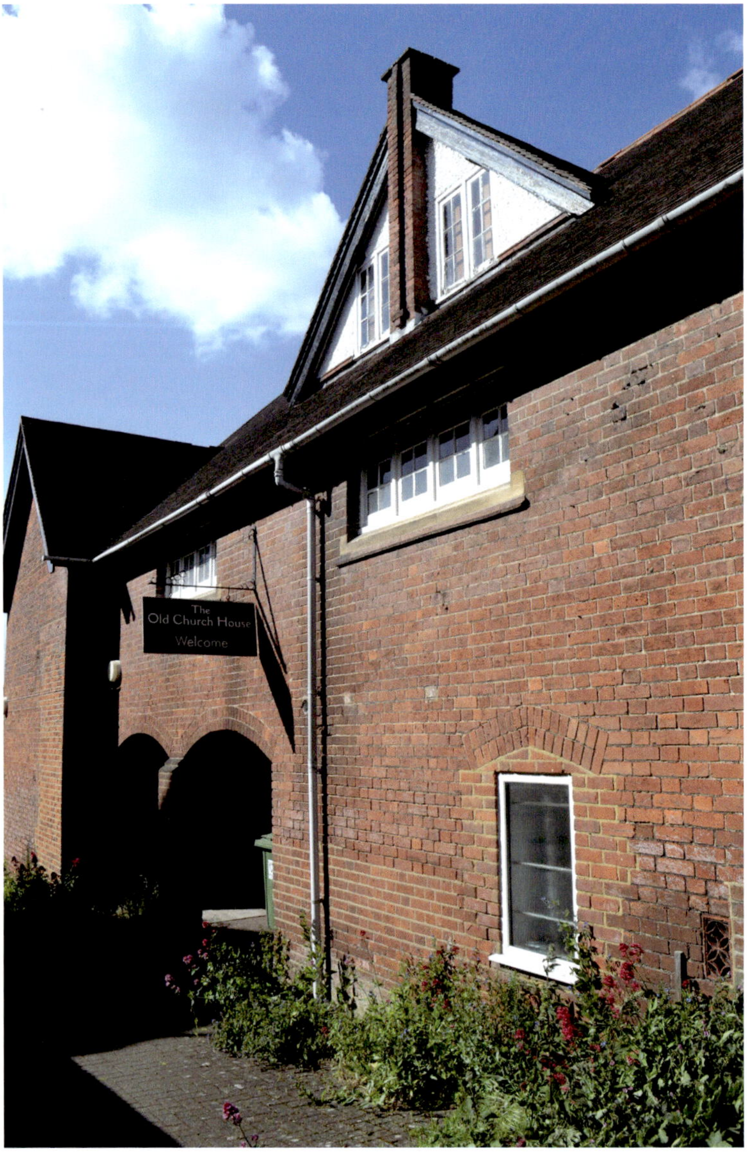

The Old Church House, completed in 1896.

40. The Market House, High Street

As a market town with a charter of 1315, it is no surprise that Tring has had a Market House for many centuries and well before 1650. The original one stood in front of the parish church. It was described as 'the old house called the Market House with the court loft over ... containing two rooms or shops below stairs, with an entry and staircase up into the court loft used for keeping of the courts, bounded South with the Market Street and the churchyard North.' It certainly suggested that Tring market already had some importance, because many small marketplaces had no market house. As a committee room standing on wooden piers, it was a form characteristic of its time and type. By 1819, it was described as 'a mean edifice on wooden pillars having a pillory and cage underneath'. Anyone found wandering the streets heavily under the influence of alcohol could end up spending the night locked in the cage.

By the end of the nineteenth century, plans were afoot to demolish the old building and construct a new one. This gave the benefit of opening up the view of the church. The New Market House, as it became known, was to be built as a memorial to Queen Victoria's Silver Jubilee of 1897. The building was to be funded primarily by public subscription, but also benefitted from a substantial contribution from Lord Rothschild. Three architects were invited to submit plans according to the *Bucks Herald* of 11 June 1898. The successful architect, of course, was Lord Rothschild's architect, William Huckvale. Progress was considerable and by 19 August 1899, the building was virtually complete and

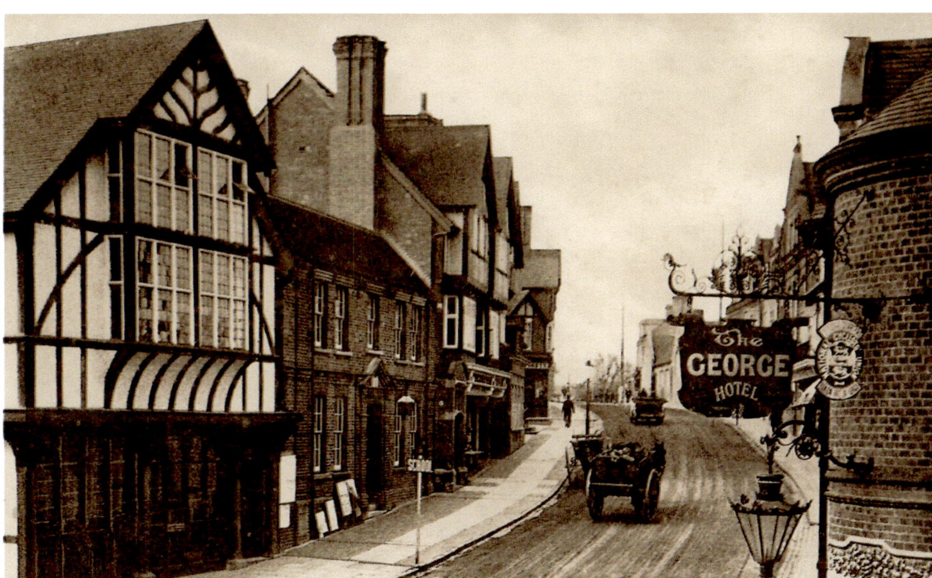

High Street, with the Market House to the left and the George Hotel opposite, now a Costa Coffee.

certainly an improvement on the previous market house. It was eventually agreed that the Urban District Council should now have responsibility for the New Market House. The ground floor of the building had an open ground floor for market stalls, with tolls payable to the council.

However, within ten years, it was decided to convert the lower area of the building into a fire brigade station. The small Vestry Hall near the church, which had housed the fire engine for many years, was now deemed too small. Tenders were sought and it was Messrs Honour & Son who were successful, submitting an estimate of £130. The *Bucks Herald* on 8 October 1910 reported that all work was now complete and despite it being an improvement, it was regretted that 'the original design of an old English open market place has been sacrificed.' Above the fire station, the rooms were used for public meetings and council meetings, as well as a variety of lectures. During the First World War, the rooms served as a boys' school as their High Street school had been commandeered to house some of the 3,000 soldiers stationed at Halton.

Eventually, once again, the fire brigade outgrew the lower premises with fire engines considerably larger. A new station was built in Brook Street, and in 1994 the ground floor of the Market House was 'reopened'. Standing on a prominent corner of the High Street, much of the building that Huckvale designed still remains to this day and is one of his finest achievements in Tring.

The Market House. The fire siren was in the bell tower on the roof.

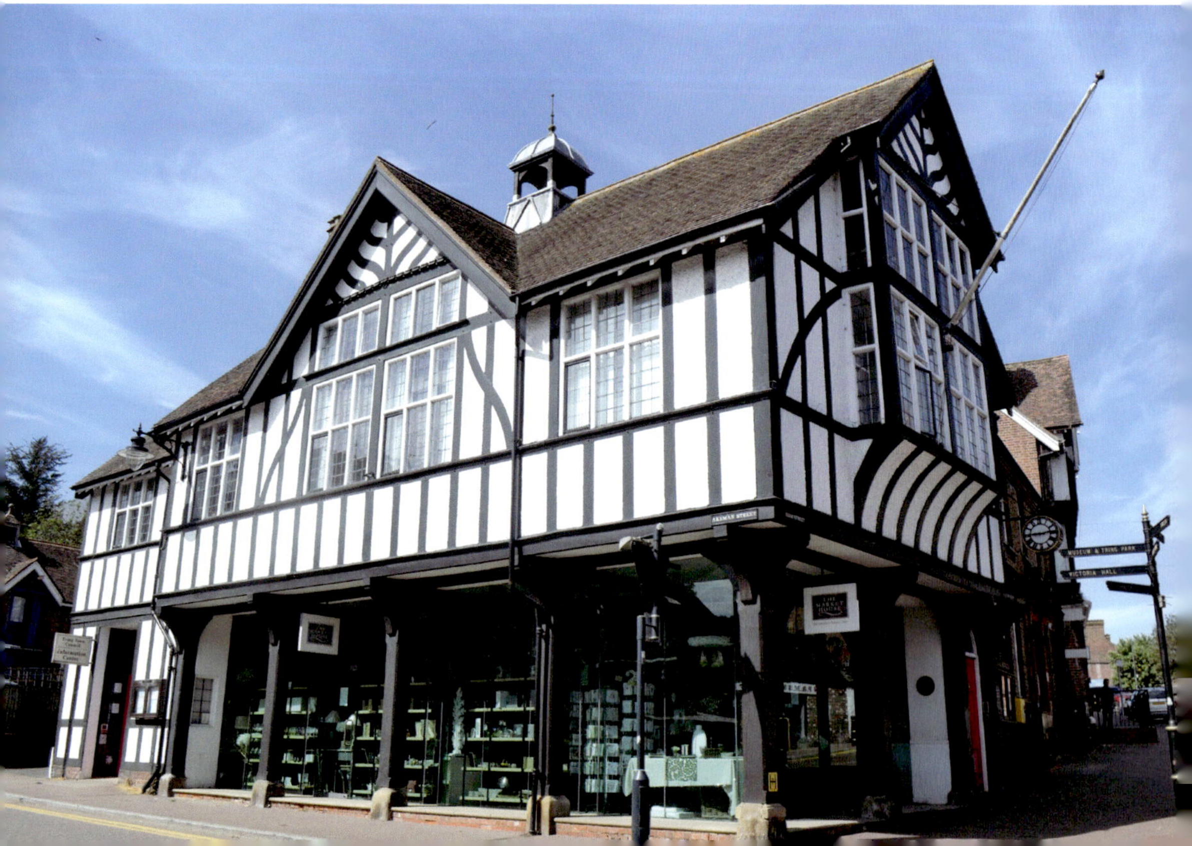

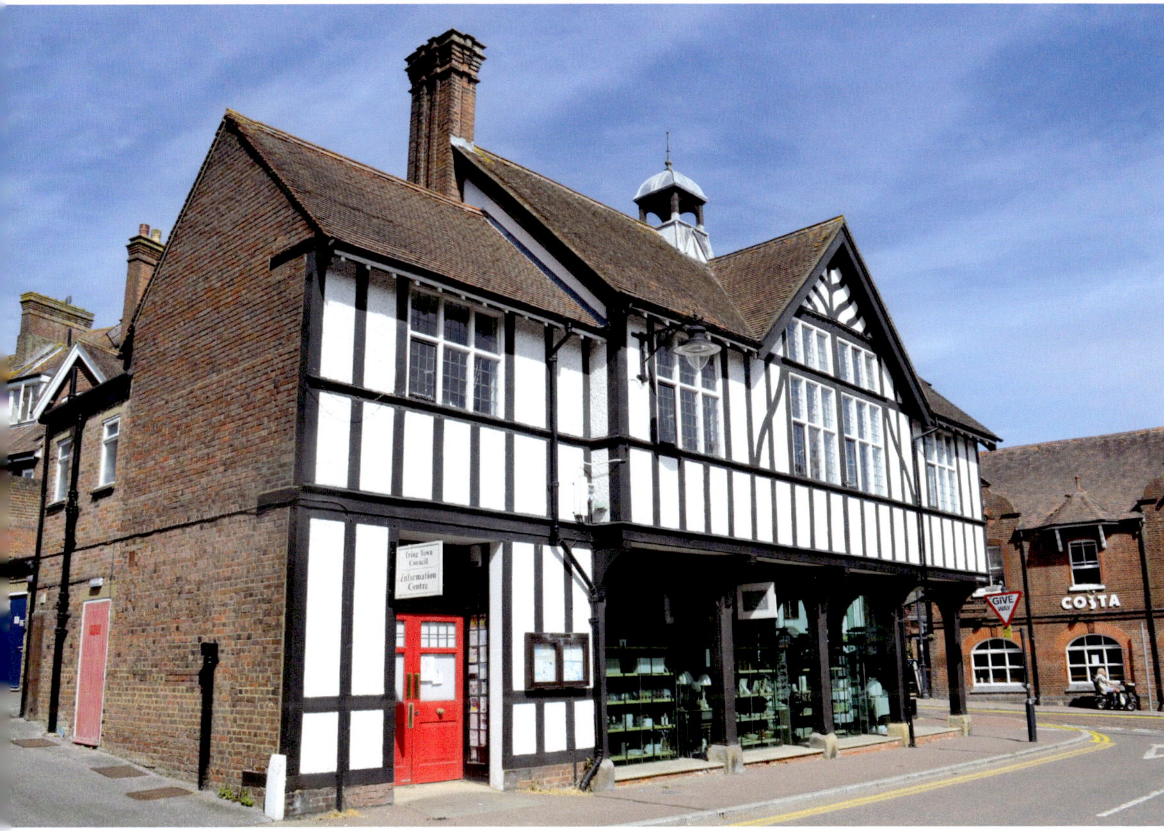

The Market House, which replaced an earlier market house nearby.

41. The Counting House

There are five structures which were built or altered for Lord Rothschild between 1891 and 1908, and form a striking group as you enter the town from the east. They include No. 8, No. 9 (listed), Nos 10 and 11 (listed), with an eighteenth-century rear wing, the Rose and Crown Inn and Nos 16 and 17 (listed). No. 8 was home to Lady Rothschild's secretary whilst No. 9 is the former Tring Park estate office and gate lodge, and included a counting house with a protected safe for estate business. They were built in the patron's characteristic domestic revival style, with red brick, timber framing, gables, windows with wooden frames and leaded lights, and monumental chimney stacks, although Nos 16 and 17 are in roughcast.

Nos 9, 10 and 11 form a pair either side of the discreet north entrance to Tring Park, and are by Huckvale. They are in part adaptations of earlier buildings rather than entirely new ones. They have distinctive tile-hanging and oriel windows with quarrels (lozenge-shaped leaded lights). The former gates across the drive were cut up for scrap at the beginning of the Second World War.

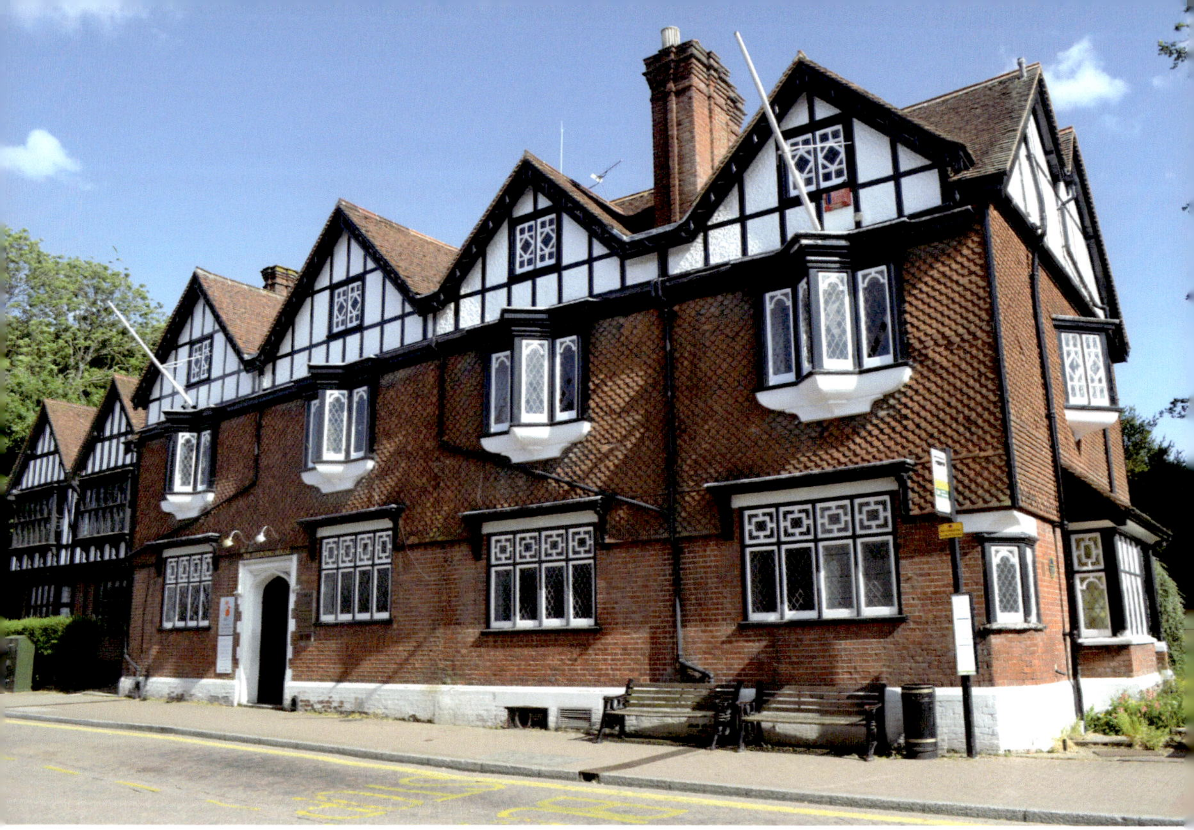

Above: The former Counting House built for Lord Rothschild.

Below: A variety of pretty oriel windows.

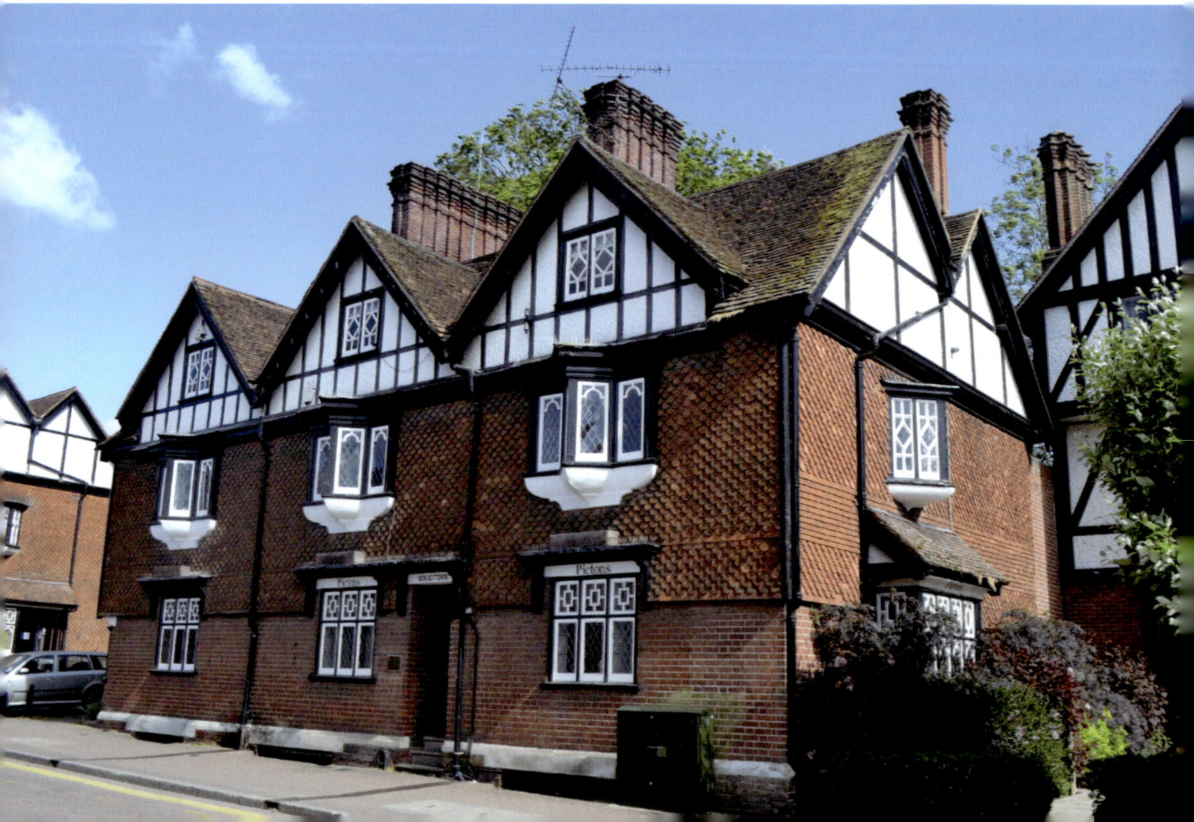

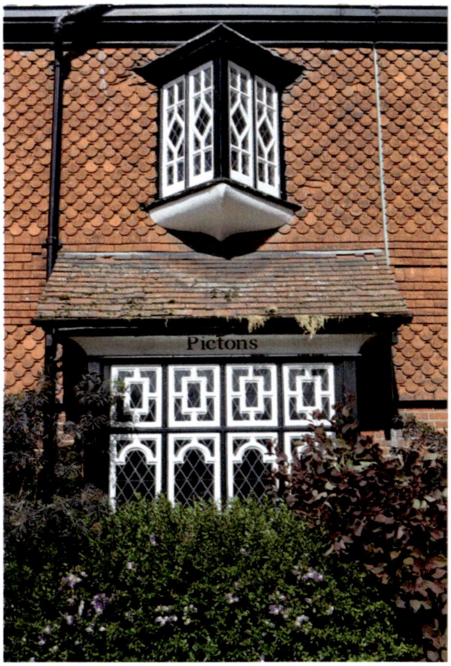

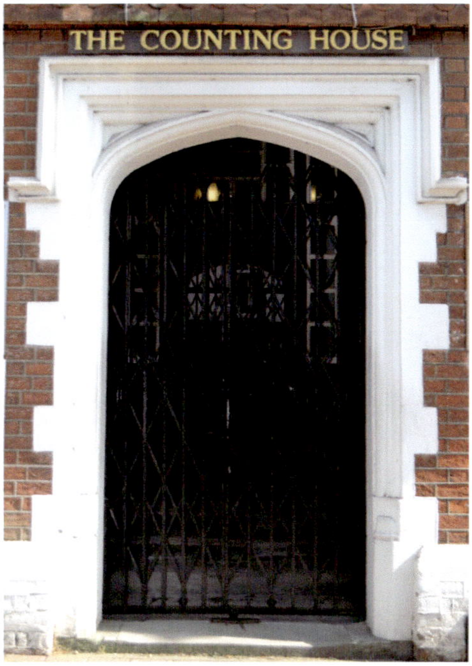

Above left: Picturesque windows on this beautiful building.

Above right: A reminder of its past use.

42. The Former Rose and Crown Hotel

The former Rose and Crown Hotel replaces an old coaching inn that was located level with the buildings on either side, which served coaches like the 'Good Intent' and the 'King William', which plied the roads between London, Aylesbury, Oxford and beyond. It was certainly a substantial building for the time. The 1891 census indicates Jabez Thorn, aged seventy-one years old, as the landlord, living with Caroline, his sixty-six-year-old wife. Jesse Thorn, their twenty-six-year-old son, was present and assisting them in the running of the inn and eventually took over as landlord. Jesse was certainly on hand to assist when nearby Home Farm caught fire, the home of Mr Richardson Carr, Lord Rothschild's agent. The *Bucks Herald* reported on the fire of 5 February 1895 that 'notwithstanding his own problems Mr Carr sent down to the Rose and Crown for hot coffee and other concomitants of a hurried breakfast. Mr Jesse Thorn, on receiving his orders, lost no time and as quickly as possible all hands at the fire were furnished with a substantial meal.'

In 1903, in response to declining fortunes in the town's economy, Lord Rothschild announced his intention to rebuild the medieval Rose and Crown Hotel. The *Bucks Herald* of 7 January 1905 stated that the plans for the new hotel had been passed but explained that the present building would not be pulled

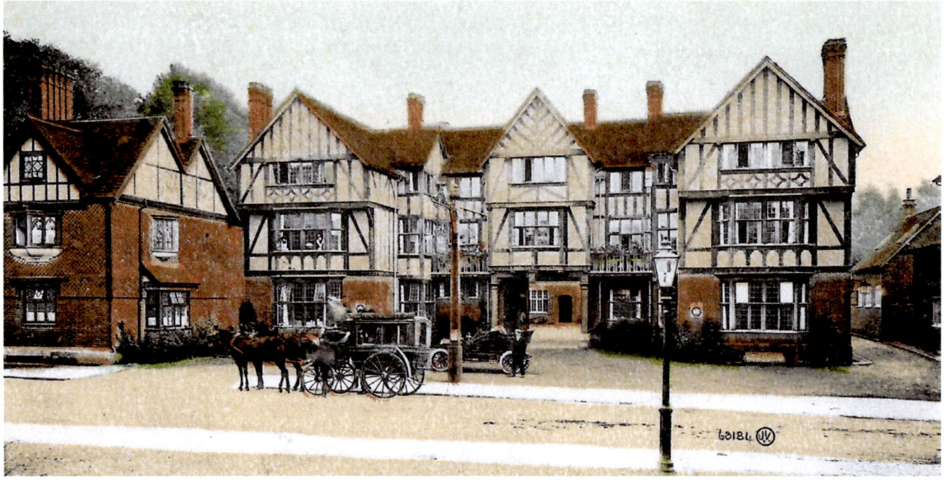

Above: The old Rose and Crown, a hotel for many years.

Below: The motor car age and the hotel thrives.

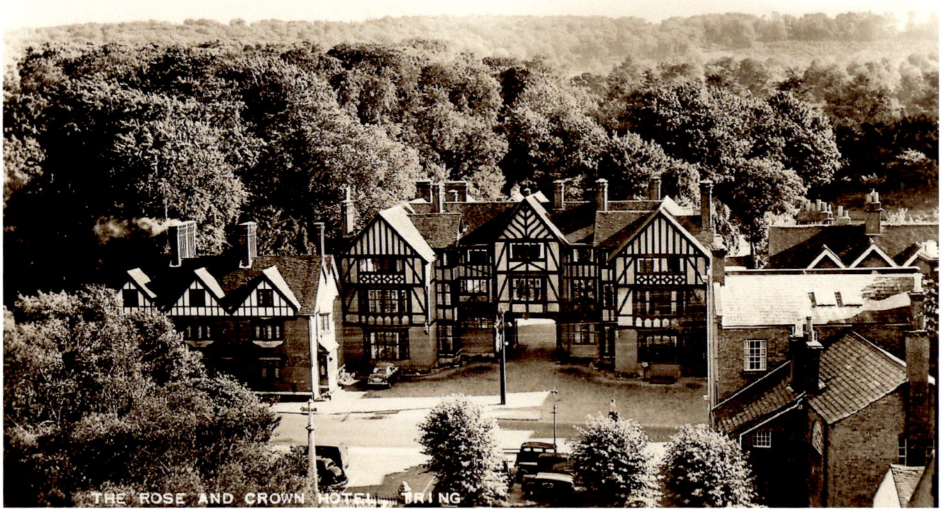

down until the new hotel was completed. To make the site as wide as possible, three shops on the west side of the old building were also demolished.

Completed in 1906, to the designs of Huckvale with an imposing Tudor Revival façade well set back from the road, it was promptly handed over to the Hertfordshire Public House Trust, an organisation promoted by Albert, 4th Earl Grey, to push back against the ill effects of drink and the monopoly power of brewers, buying and building inns giving a greater prominence to healthier activities with added sporting facilities, such as tennis, squash, a bowling green and rifle shooting. It was the forerunner of Trust House Forte. It was occasionally used by visitors to the nearby mansion, including Edward, Prince of Wales, in 1935.

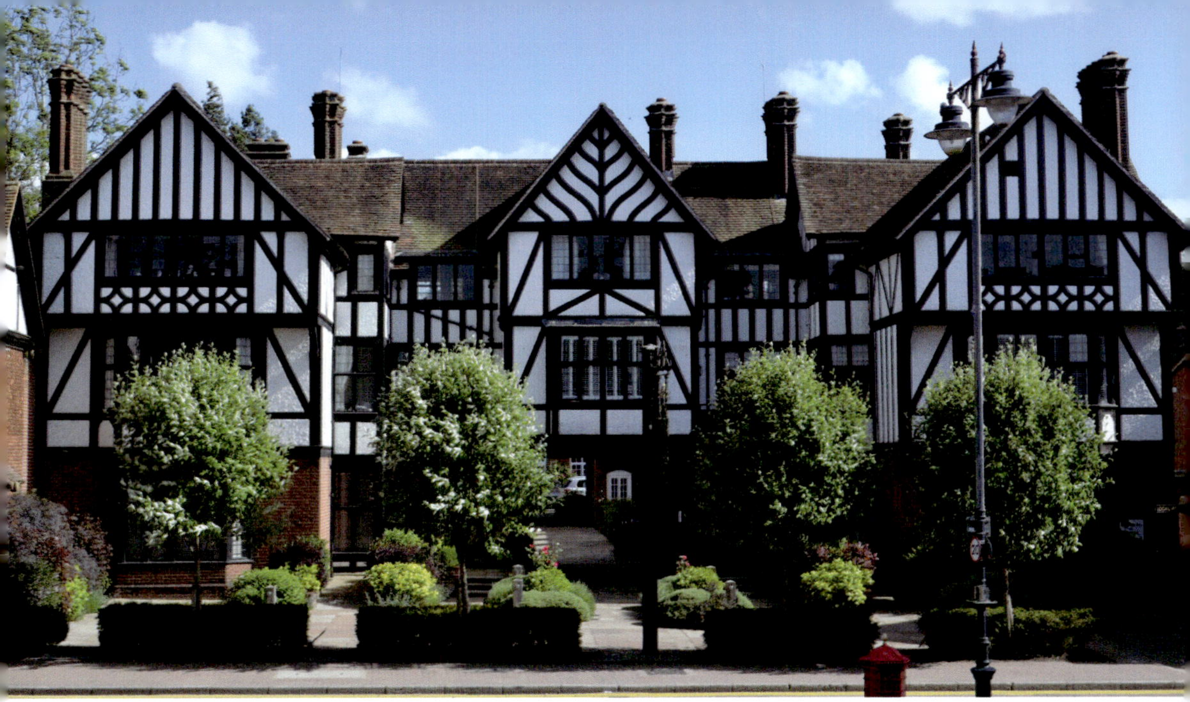

Above: No longer a hotel but converted into residential units.

Right: A fine Tudor Revival building designed by Huckvale.

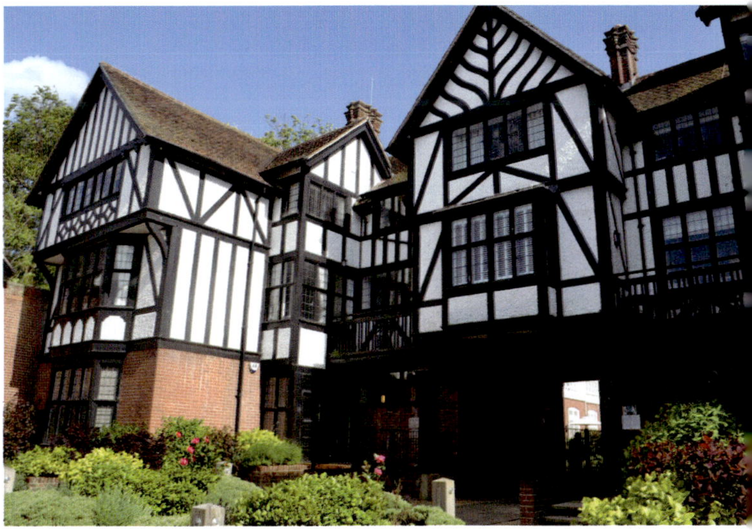

As the motor car became more popular, early in the twentieth century, the Rose and Crown became a favourite gathering point for cars and motorcycles on their way to Aston Hill climbing events, with over forty vehicles often parking in front of the hotel. The hotel remained until the need for such hotels in the centre of country towns had almost disappeared, with motorists preferring out-of-town travel lodges with parking facilities and standard accommodation. It eventually closed and today has been converted into residential units. This author has fond memories of staying here in the early 1990s as a guest of Tring-based Civic Trees, when he was a humble landscape architect inspecting trees for a housing regeneration project in Carlisle.

43. The Black Horse, Frogmore Street

The public house we know today as The Black Horse is not the original one that stood in this location. The old Black Horse was demolished in the early 1900s and was rebuilt and remains a popular public house today. In the 1841 census at Frogmore End, the only residents listed were Alfred Chapman, a twenty-five-year-old labourer and his wife, Ann. By the 1851 census, Alfred was named as a 'Beer and lodging house keeper' with his wife, who was listed as a 'victualler', two servants and twenty-two lodgers. These lodgers were a mixed bunch of people, ranging from a baby born in Tring to a seventy-eight-year-old Thomas Clowes, a collier from Cocknell in Cheshire. Others included seventy-six-year-old Charles Johnson, a grinder and tinker from Rugby, two men from Ireland, one a blacksmith and the other a door mat hawker. Also listed was a roving musician from Italy. Two families were also lodging here, each with a husband and wife and with three children. Old records indicate a substantial building, and it was never described as overcrowded.

The 1861 census records James Abraham as a 'lodging house keeper and fellmonger' with his wife Harriet and nineteen lodgers. Harriet died a few years later and by 1871, James was living with twelve lodgers, a 'lodging housekeeper' by the name of Charlotte Hedges. In 1881, Edmond Collyer was described as 'a publican and lodging house keeper' with his wife, Matilda, six children ranging from six months to seventeen years old. There were still many lodgers present, up to twenty-one still residing here. By 1891, the pub was called The Old Black Horse with fifty-five-year-old John Archer from Wilstone described as 'a beerhouse keeper'.

The Black Horse at the bottom of Frogmore Street.

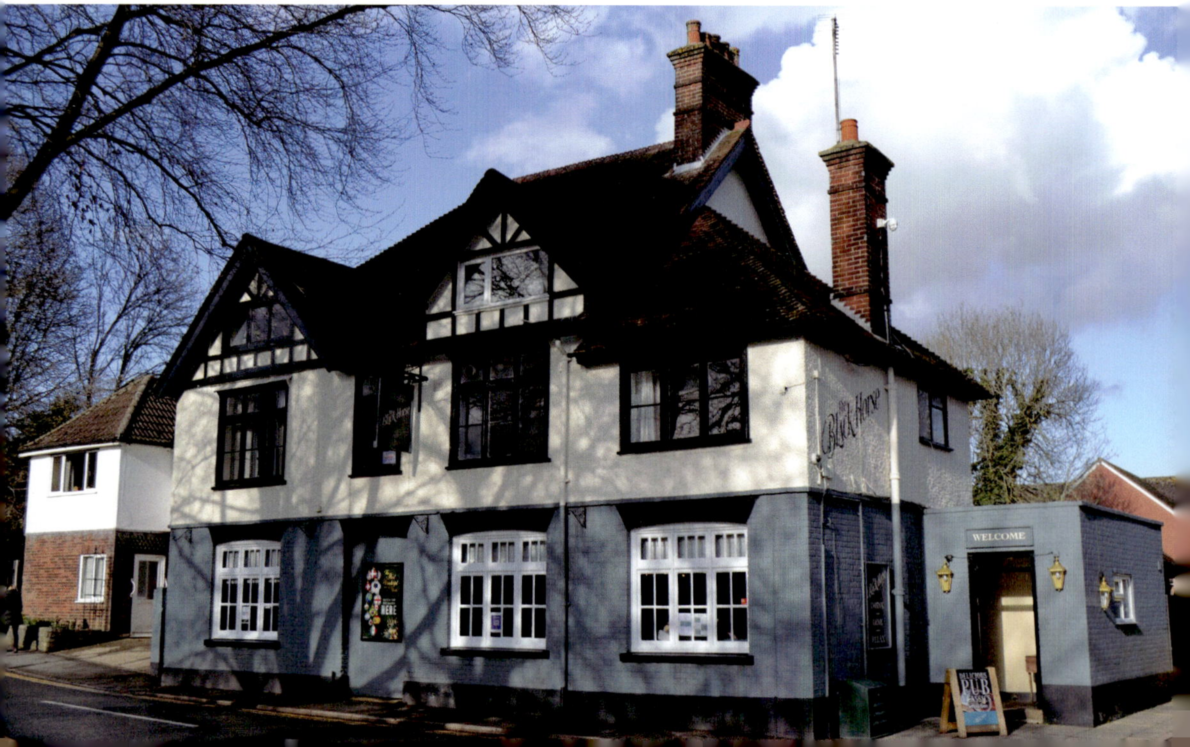

Reports in local newspapers of the time have often described a number of public affrays in many of the public houses in Tring involving fighting and drunkenness. The Old Black Horse was no different. In the *Bucks Herald* of 16 November 1895 it was recorded that 'a man who gave the name of Henry Marsh deliberately smashed a window in the Black Horse in Frogmore Street. He was arrested and the next morning was taken before Captain Cooper who sentenced him to 14 days imprisonment'. On 20 July 1907, the *Bucks Herald* reported 'breach of the peace – at the Berkhamsted Session on Wednesday Herbert Budd of Tring and George Eggleton of Wigginton were summoned to answer a charge of breaking the peace by fighting on the 6th inst. PC Gregory spoke of finding the two men fighting in the Bell Inn yard with from 50 to 100 men round them. Witness separated them and got Budd to go home but Eggleton used bad language towards him and tried to get more beer, first at the Bell, and afterwards at the Robin Hood. The case was adjourned for a fortnight.'

44. Former Unity Hall, Lower High Street

Tring's first cinema opened in 1912 and was located on the Lower High Street and was known as the Gem Cinema. The Unity Hall was above the Tring Co-op and held 300 people, with a 19-foot-deep stage. It was frequently used for plays. Many alterations were made and it became the Gem picture hall, with P. J. Darvell as the licensee. It was Darvell who built the new Gem cinema in Western Road,

Unity Hall, once one of several cinemas in the town.

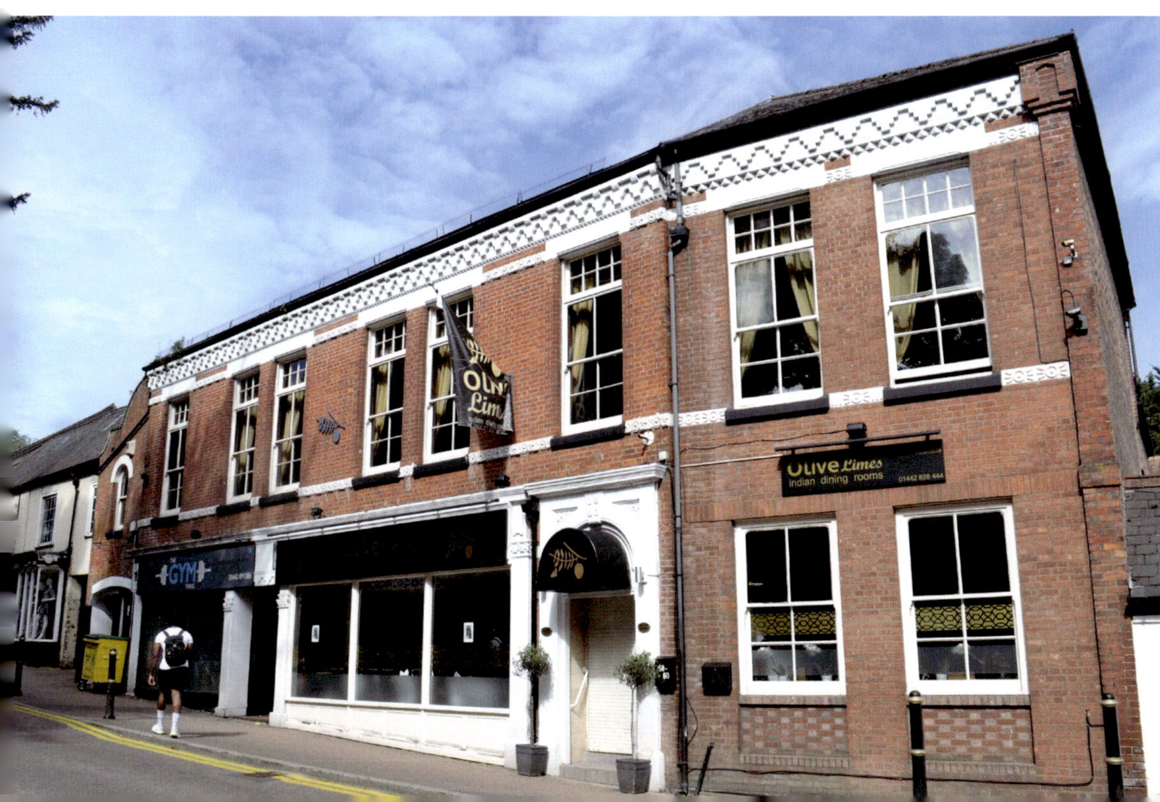

but unfortunately this did not survive for very long, with the new Empire cinema being built in Akeman Street. The Gem closed in the early 1920s. The name Unity Hall is still visible to this day.

45. Tring Police Station

The County Council purchased a vacant plot in the centre of the town in 1912. It had previously been occupied by a butcher's shop and abattoir. The well-known Tring firm of builders, Honours, built it for £893, and it opened in January 1914. It is the oldest station still in use in Hertfordshire. Designed by a Hertfordshire County Council architect, it was originally the home of the constable and his family, with one of the ground floor front rooms being the guardroom, where the public entered. At the time of its construction, there was criticism of the new building in the *Bucks Herald* of 13 September 1913. 'This latest addition to the architectural features of the town has been this week thrown open to view by the removal of hoarding which had hither to hidden it. Built of dull yellow bricks faced with red, it is a severe and business-like building doubtless admirably adapted for the purpose for which it was erected. But it scarcely harmonises with the adjacent buildings or adds to the beauty of that part of the High Street. Perhaps the county council did not wish to make it too attractive.'

The police station, still in operation today.

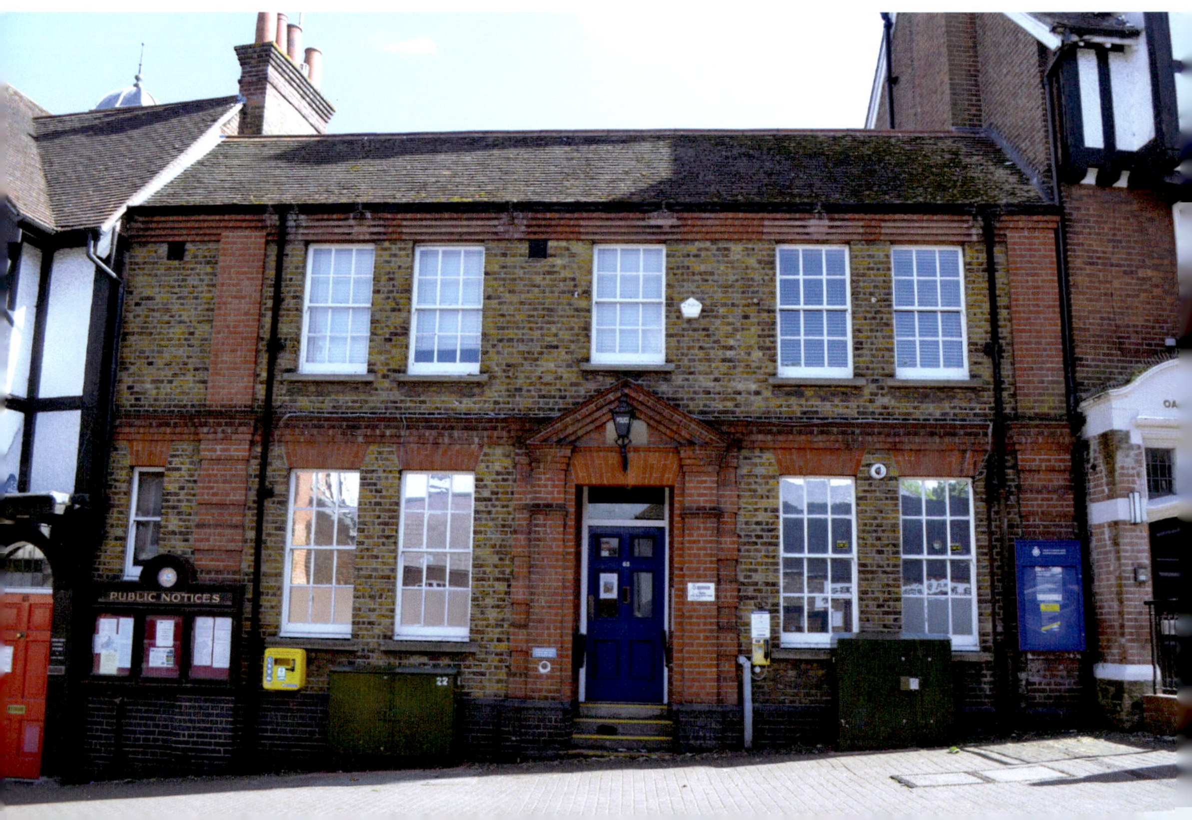

The other front room used to be the kitchen, but all that remains of that now is a traditional pantry with a fly screen. A small back room, once the family parlour, is now the interview room of the station. No cell remains, although a small area used as an exercise yard is still there, with a high-level glazed skylight.

Plans show where the 13 feet by 9 feet cell and its single bed would have been. Still in occasional use are the outdoor dog kennels. When stray dogs are picked up, they are housed there until the Dacorum Dog Warden can collect them. The rooms upstairs, originally bedrooms, are well lit and comfortable, and are now used as offices for the police force. There was a redevelopment in 1937 when an extension was built to provide a bathroom and indoor toilet.

The policemen in the nineteenth century had to be fit to get about as they were all 'on foot' even if they were called to one of the surrounding villages. If there was an emergency, a fast runner, usually a small boy, came to the police station to summon help. Horses were never used, but later bicycles enabled faster communication. Reaching the scene was not always straightforward. The Valetta aeroplane that crashed in the woods at Tom's Hill in Aldbury in 1954 was not found for half an hour, by which time sixteen RAF men had perished. It was that incident that stimulated the development of an emergency kit for extraordinary events.

This, of course, was not the first police station in the town. Before that, Vestry Hall in Church Lane was used between 1866 and 1913. There could not have been much crime in those days, because there was only one permanent constable, and the building also housed the town's horse-drawn fire engine.

The first known building to be used by the constabulary was the town's original Market House, believed to have dated from the 1650s. This building stood on the High Street, directly in front of St Peter & St Paul's Church and consisted of a large trading hall on wooden stilts. A cage and pillory were located underneath. When the Market Hall and cage were demolished in July 1900, the date 1680 was found carved into an internal beam. Today the site of the former Market House is an open space known as Church Square.

46. The Former Empire Picture Theatre, Akeman Street

Like many towns the size of Tring, townsfolk were able to visit a local purpose-built cinema to enjoy the film industry's latest releases. In February 1958, public film shows ceased in Tring when the Regal closed suddenly and unexpectedly. The cinema was reopened by another proprietor shortly after, but closed again in March 1960, bringing to an end almost fifty years of cinema in Tring. One of the more successful cinemas, however, was the Empire, later to become the Gaiety on Akemen Street. The *Bucks Herald* of 12 February 1916 reported: 'THE COUNCIL'S COTTAGES. A letter was read from Mr. James Honour, saying that he had sold four cottages in Akeman-street to a Cinema Company. As the company required the site, the tenants would have to get out. He asked if the

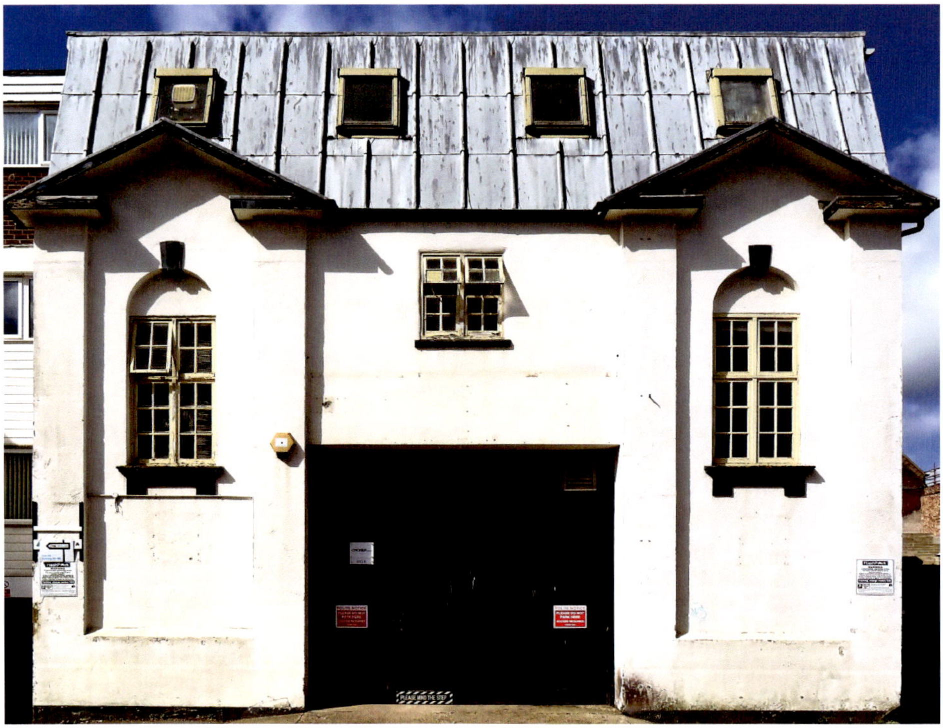

A former cinema, the Empire Picture Theatre, also known as the Gaiety. (© Snapshooter46)

Council would allow them to move into the Council cottages. They were good tenants and respectable.–The Council regretted that they were unable to accede to his request. The question had been raised before, but they could not do it. It was contrary to the conditions under which they held the property.'

The cottages were eventually freed of their tenants, demolished, and the building of a new picture house pressed ahead on the now vacant site. By July construction was almost complete: 'THE NEW CINEMA.–The new Cinematograph Theatre in Akeman-street, now nearly completed, will be opened in the course of the week. The building has an imposing front designed in the Georgian style, and the interior has been very tastefully decorated in the Adams period. The ventilation is of the most modern principle, with Boyle's patent roof ventilators, and, in addition, an electric exhaust fan. The heating will be by means of gas radiators, and other features, such as tip-up seats, are included to add to the comfort of theatre-goers. Two dressing rooms are placed in conjunction to the stage, which is designed for variety turns of a refined class. No expense has been spared to make this theatre the last word in Cinemas. The Building has been carried out by the well-known firm of J. Honour and Son Ltd., for a local syndicate, from the plans and under the personal supervision of Mr. Fred Taylor A.R.I.B.A., architect, Aylesbury,' reported the *Bucks Herald* of 22 July 1916.

The Empire was a purpose-built cinema designed to seat 250 people, plus a small balcony with sixty-four seats. The architect designed the building to the requirements of William Charles Taylor, who was determined to open before the new Gem in Western Road; in that he succeeded, for the Empire opened on Saturday 29 July 1916, two days before the Gem.

By August 1931 the Empire had been renamed the Gaiety, and as such the cinema continued in business until 1937, its last advertised film programme appearing in the 23 April edition of the *Bucks Herald*. Despite the lack of programme advertising the cinema appears to have continued in some form, for positions for a cashier and two attendants were advertised in August. There followed a couple of charity functions held on the premises following which the Gaiety disappears from view. It was likely that the town could not support two picture houses with the newly built Regal now serious competition. Several changes of ownership occurred over the next few years but all with limited success.

By December 1939 the building was advertised to let, as being 'suitable for factory or storage purposes'. In January 1947 the *Bucks Herald* announced that the cinema building was to become 'a small factory for turning out high-grade toys'.

The former picture house, although much altered, still stands in Akeman Street, having the distinction of being the only one of Tring's three purpose-built cinemas to have escaped the demolition ball. The building in March 2023 was under refurbishment.

47. Great West Plantation, Duckmore Lane

Hidden away on Duckmore Lane is a house and office, designed by local architect, Alan Tye. Great West Plantation was built on land formerly owned by the Rothschild family. On an area rich with mature trees, a simplistic T-shape

House and office by architect Alan Tye.

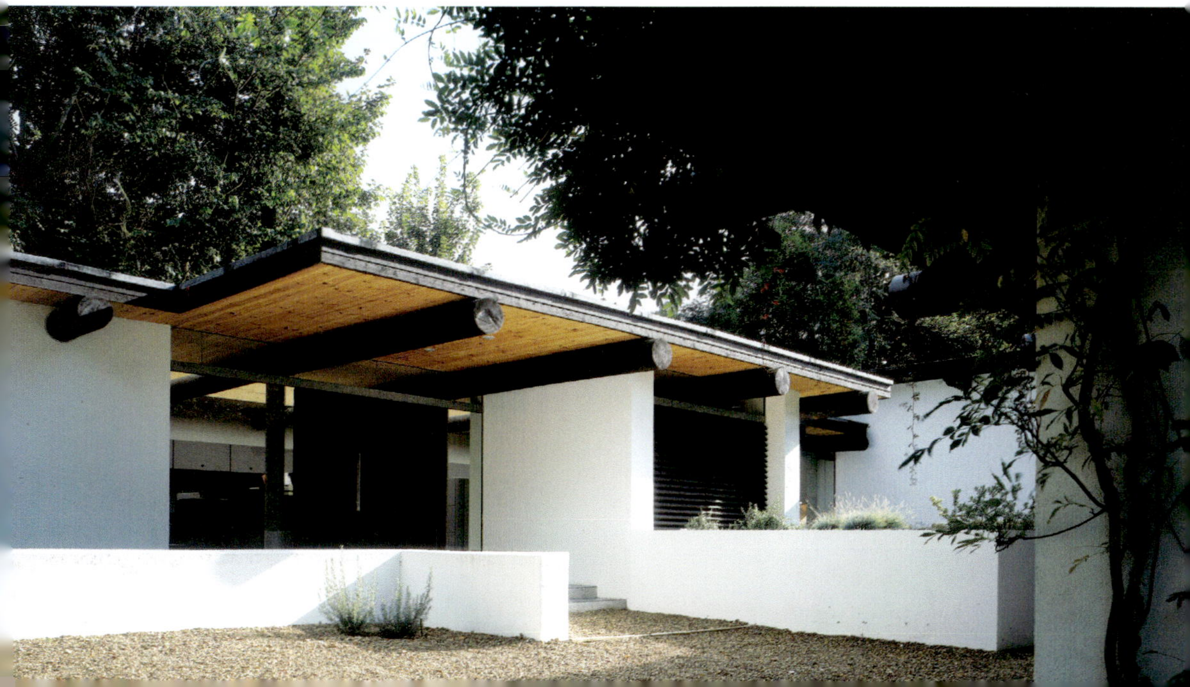

structure was built with external white-rendered concrete walls and a flat roof supported by exposed brown tree trunks. The most striking feature of the property is a double-height full-width window influenced by Le Corbusier's Pavilion de l'Esprit Nouveau (1925). The main house was built in 1975 and in 1992 an award-winning office extension was added, in keeping with the original architectural vernacular.

Pevsner describes it as a 'flat-roofed, T-Plan house and office … hidden in a plantation of trees'. The *Architectural Review*, in October 1976, describes it as 'Exhibiting a low-key, almost folksy modernity, it derives from the Danish strand of the Modern Movement.'

48. The David Evans Court Theatre

The David Evans Court Theatre was originally established as The Pendley Arts Centre and is housed in a converted 'French barn' which dates back exactly 100 years from the date the theatre first opened in 1978.

This once derelict building stands not far from Tring station on the edge of the Pendley Manor estate, which was formerly the family home of famous equestrian and BBC's 'voice of showjumping' Dorian Williams (1914–85). He used it as an indoor riding school, although at one time it housed an indoor tennis court, hence the theatre's name. Williams was a keen amateur actor and in 1949 founded the

Converted into offices.

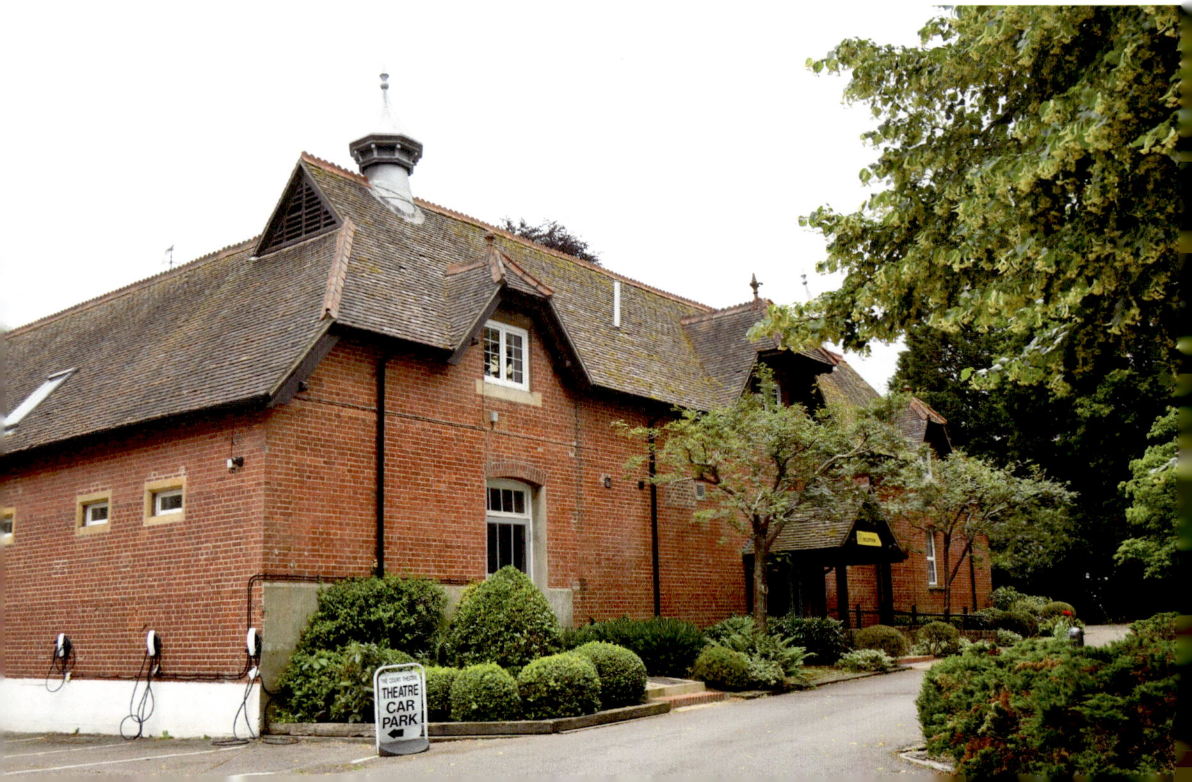

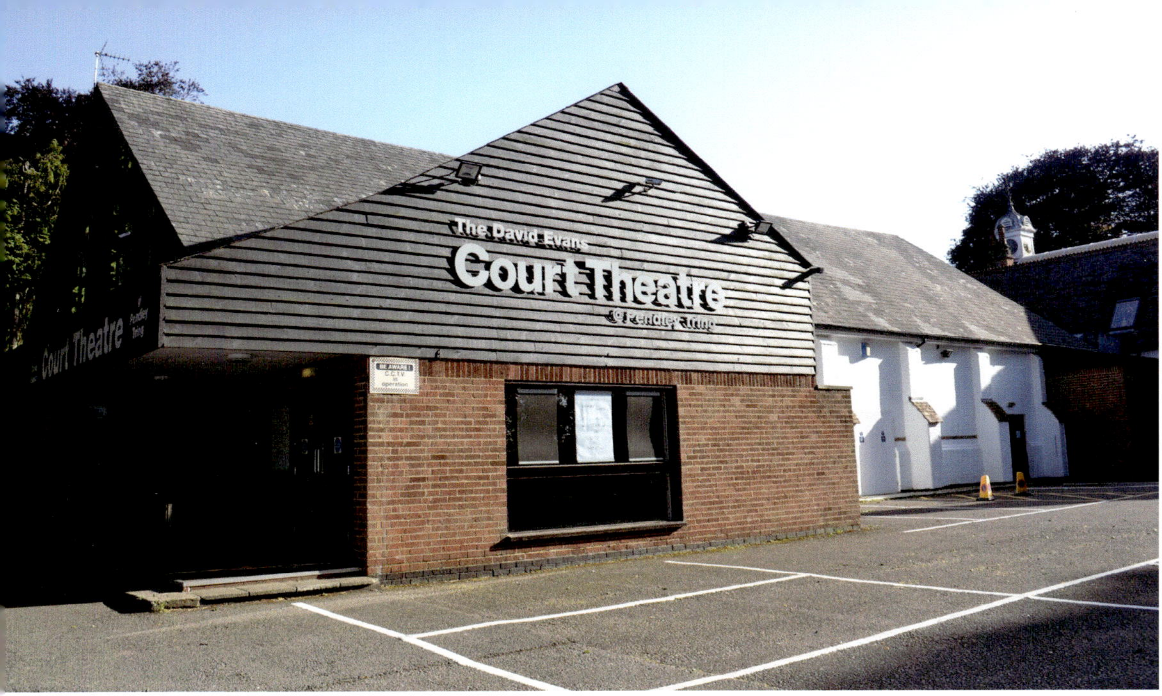

A popular community facility today on the edge of Tring.

popular Pendley Open Air Shakespeare Festival, which still takes place annually each summer in the manor grounds.

The estate, including the theatre, changed hands in 1985 when it became the headquarters of The Grass Roots Group, a leading provider of employee and customer engagement solutions headed up by the company founder and chairman, David Evans. In 1987 the manor house was purchased by an independent hotelier and became, as it is today, The Pendley Manor Hotel. The Grass Roots Group relocated themselves into the theatre complex and adjoining stables, which were converted into offices in the same year. For many years the theatre ran as a community venue under the ownership, patronage and support of The Grass Roots Group and its founder David Evans, the first recipient of an MBE for his achievements in corporate social responsibility in 2008.

In 2016 when the holding company was acquired by Blackhawk Network Inc and moved out of the premises, the building and theatre were purchased by David Evans with the purpose of housing his many businesses and philanthropic endeavours, thus ensuring the future of this historic building and its wonderful community-run theatre.

49. Corpus Christi Catholic Church

This is a relatively new church, but it incorporates the footprint and some fabric from the predecessor church. Designed by architect Anthony Delarue, he wrote that the 'design brings together several traditions of brick construction – the Classical Roman basilica, the English Renaissance and local rural tradition'.

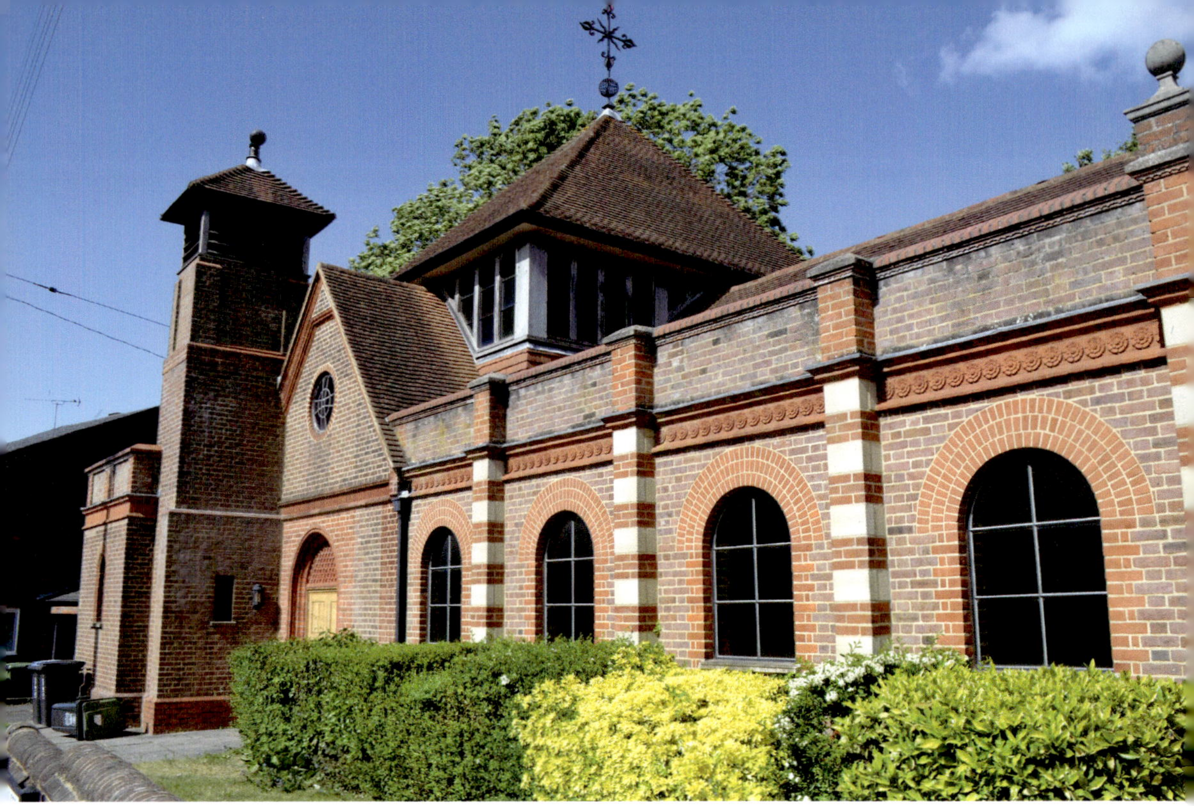

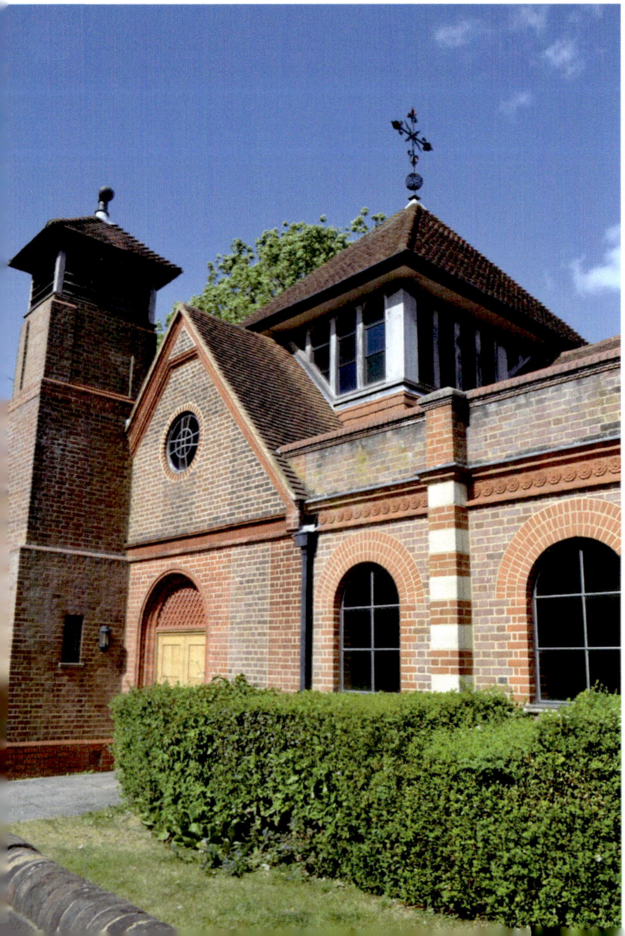

Above: Corpus Christi Catholic Church, bringing together a number of design elements.

Left: An award-winning building, deservedly so.

The first church at Tring was built by Fr Henry Hardy, an Anglican convert and descendant of Captain Hardy of Trafalgar fame, who also built churches at Berkhamsted, Boxmoor and Rickmansworth (qv). Fr Hardy's church was a small gabled brick structure with a bell turret over the entrance. According to a local newspaper account quoted in the parish history, it was built by a Mr C. Green of Boxmoor (the general form of the building, with the ridge lowered to accommodate the belfry, bears some resemblance to Fr Hardy's earlier church at Boxmoor).

Although modestly augmented over the years, the 1912 church was increasingly inadequate for the growing parish, and plans were advanced for its substantial enlargement as early as the 1960s. The tower and side aisle were added from designs by George Mathers in the 1960s. It was not until 1995 that Anthony Delarue was appointed and real progress was made towards the building of a new church. His scheme retained the tower and outer walls, or at least the footprint, of the old church except on the west side, which was opened up to a new aisled nave (on the site of the old presbytery). The main axis was thus turned around by 180 degrees, with the former sanctuary becoming a baptistery and Lady Chapel, and the tabernacle placed in a recess in the former aisle. The first Mass was celebrated in the new church on 11 November 1999 and the building was consecrated by Archbishop Murphy O'Connor on 16 February 2001. The design won a craftsmanship award from the Brick Development Association.

In 2012 a new parish office was added alongside the sacristy, designed to be in keeping with Delarue's work (architects Kyle Smart Associates of Dunstable).

50. Tring School

The teaching of older schoolchildren at Mortimer Hill began as early as 1949 but facilities were very basic with only a few huts present and children still being taught at the old school on the High Street. In 1953, it was decided to replace the huts with a purpose-built Secondary Modern School on Mortimer Hill. The building was completed in about three years by local firm Donald Lockhart, and was eventually in use in early 1957 with further additions over the years. The latest project has been the £30 million project, largely government-funded, to rebuild Tring School on this well-established site.

The new building was constructed by Bowmer and Kirkland and it is now one of the most sustainably designed schools in the country, with additional facilities to support the pastoral care and emotional well-being of the students from Tring and surrounding area. After years of planning and then building, the students and staff of Tring School moved into their new building in January 2022.

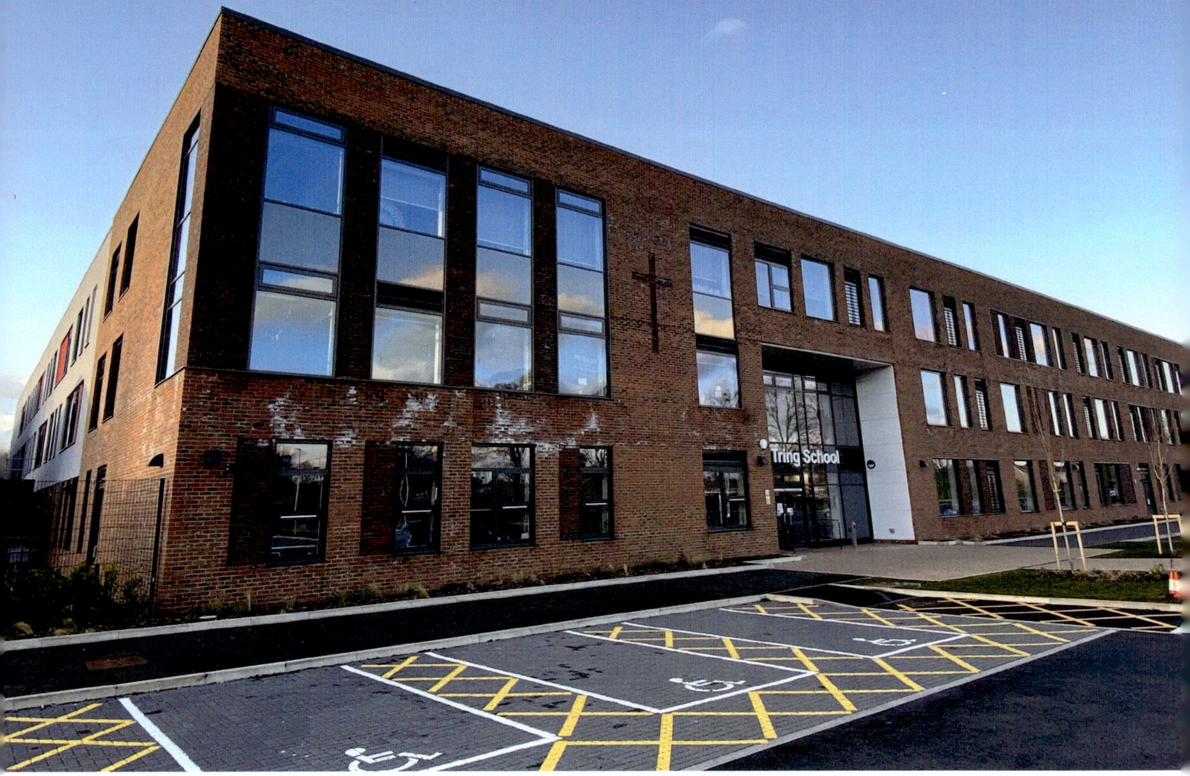

Above: Tring School, sustainable modern architecture.

Below: Opened in early 2022.

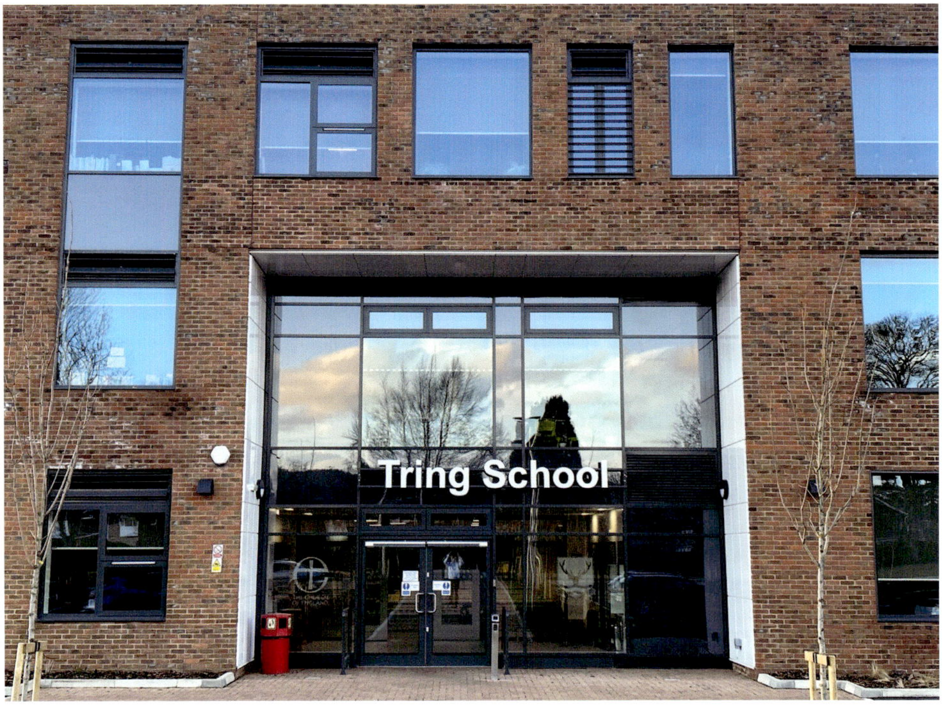

Bibliography

http://kingsarmstring.co.uk/history/

https://tringlocalhistory.org.uk/Recollections_2/index.htm

https://tringlocalhistory.org.uk/Silk_Mill/index.htm

https://newmillbaptist.org.uk/nmbc/wp-content/uploads/2017/04/NewMillHistory.pdf

https://taking-stock.org.uk/building/tring-corpus-christi/

https://courttheatre.co.uk/history/

https://www.prisonhistory.org/2020/02/lock-ups-in-tring-hertfordshire/

https://tringlocalhistory.org.uk/Cinema/index.htm

Bass, Mike, and Fowler, Jill, *Around Tring* (Nonsuch Publishing Ltd, Stroud, 2006)

Bass, Mike, and Fowler, Jill, *Around Tring* (Tempus Publishing Ltd, Stroud, 2001)

Bettley, James, Pevsner, Nikolaus, and Cherry, Bridget, *The Buildings of England: Hertfordshire* (Yales University Press, London, 2019)

Fowler, Jill, *Tring Through Time* (Amberley Publishing, Stroud, 2009)

Fowler, Jill, *Tring 1951–2000 – Images of England* (Tempus Publishing, Stroud, 2008)

Fowler, Jill, *Ten Tring Public Houses* (The Tring and District Local History and Museum Society, 2015)

Fowler, Jill, *Ten Local Landmarks* (The Tring and District Local History and Museum Society, 2014)

Fowler, Jill, *Tring Town – A Stroll Around the Old Town* (The Tring and District Local History and Museum Society, 2016)

Little, Bob, *A Perspective on Pendley: A History of Pendley Manor* (St Albans, 2014)

Richards, Sheila, *A History of Tring* (Tring Urban District Council, 1974)

Whitaker, Allan, *Brewers in Hertfordshire, A Historical Gazetteer* (Hertfordshire Publications, 2005)

Woodhouse, Barry, *Tring – A Pictorial History* (Phillimore, Chichester, 1996)

Discover Historic Tring – Tring Heritage Trail,Tring Local History Museum

Acknowledgements

Paul Rabbitts would like to thank the Tring and District Local History and Museum Society, which has carried so much research on the history of Tring, some of it used in this publication and acknowledged by the author. In particular the research carried out by Jill Fowler, Mike Bass and especially Tim Amsden and his research on Huckvale. I would like to thank Tim Amsden in particular for his feedback. Their work has been a valuable source of material. Thanks to those people who live in many of the properties who have allowed me to photograph after knocking on doors. I would also like to thank friend and former colleague Jane Custance for coffee and cake.

About the Author

Paul Rabbitts is a Fellow of the Royal Society of Arts, as well as a Fellow of the Royal Historical Society. He has managed public parks, culture and heritage for thirty-five years for various local authorities, including Carlisle, Middlesbrough, Watford, Southend-on-Sea and Norwich. He is also a prolific author on architecture, public parks and a noted expert on the history of public parks, as well as the Victorian and Edwardian bandstand. He has written several books in the 'in 50 Buildings' series, including Watford, Leighton Buzzard, Aylesbury, Luton, Salford, Bournemouth, Windsor, Carlisle, Salisbury, Welwyn and Welwyn Garden City, Hertford and Manchester. He currently lives in Leighton Buzzard with his wife Julie and daughter Ellie.